Your Secret My Story:
The Story of Baby Mary Doe

By Kate Kendall

Disclaimer: While all the incidents in this book are true and from my viewpoints, the locations, the names, and personal characteristics of the individuals involved have been changed in order to protect their privacy. Any resulting resemblance to persons living or dead is entirely coincidental and unintentional.

Newborn Baby Girl Found Abandoned in Jefferson County

Police are searching for the mother of a newborn baby who was found abandoned in a Jefferson subdivision of Monday. Officer Green estimated the baby to be about two hours old. The baby was wrapped in a towel on top of a paper bag on the lawn of a home. Police Chief John Campbell said authorities are searching for the baby's mother.

The police never found my mother, and I have spent 25 years searching for her. To clarify, when I use the term "mother" here, I am talking about my biological parent. I *do* have a mother and a father, Patricia and James Peters - two loving, wonderful people who adopted me when I was 7-1/2 months old. To be clear, I am grateful for them, their profound love, and the life they have given me. But I also felt profound emptiness and sadness, not knowing who physically gave life to me.

At age seven, I remember sitting with my parents in the family room of our two-bedroom duplex in LaGrange, Georgia. The conversation that ensued was one that takes place in thousands of adoptive family's homes across the country every year. My father began, "sweetheart, your mother and I need to talk with you about something very important. We love you very much. You are a very special little girl, and we chose you." He continued, "You did not grow in your mother's belly. Your mother could not grow a baby in her belly." I was confused and did not understand what he was trying to tell me. But I do remember his next words, "Sweetheart, you are adopted." At the time, however, this news had little meaning for me; I just wanted to go back outside to play.

My favorite pastime was planting acorns with my dad. Right outside of our kitchen window was a huge oak tree, which he said was our special tree because we had planted the acorns that made it grow. When the weather permitted, my dad and I went outside to gather acorns. We always had several full buckets and would walk around the yard planting acorns and being silly. To this day, every time I visit my parents, I drive by that oak tree. Seeing it takes me back to my carefree childhood.

My dad, James Peters, and I have always had an exceptionally close relationship. He has been my best friend and lifelong confidant. Most of my early memories are of the two of us. My mother Patricia would observe us from the kitchen window but was not actively involved in the games we played. Another favorite activity was making a maze for my hamster, Whiskers, by standing up books together without an exit. We would watch Whiskers navigate his way to the end, where a surprise treat waited. Then there were the stories. My dad sat on my bed every night and recounted a spellbinding story. I know now that they were based on Grimms' Fairytales; however, at the time, I assumed that my amazing daddy had made them all up. He was an animated storyteller and changed voices for the characters. My favorite was about an adventurous dog named Spot who got lost one day. The simple narrative described how Spot found his way home, back to the family that loved and missed him. That story always held a special place in my heart, but I never understood why. Now I do.

I did not think again about being adopted. That is, not until my sixth-grade teacher assigned a project to create a family tree, listing family traits, ancestral heritage, and important life events. I realized that I could not even list similarities in appearance because I look nothing like my adoptive parents. My father is solid, with broad shoulders, and my mother, is rather heavy. I, on the other hand, am petite and wiry. They are both Nordic-fair, whereas I am Mediterranean-dark.

I was apprehensive about how to describe people I have never known or even worse, fabricating details. On another level, I was deeply troubled that my family tree – and therefore myself – had no roots. As always, I shared my concerns with my father, who patiently sat with me to create a family tree based on my adoptive family's history. Then he suggested that I write a paragraph explaining that I was adopted and that being chosen by my parents meant that I was extra special. Nevertheless, I was still embarrassed to present my project in class because I did not know how my friends would react. I did not like feeling different.

On the day of my presentation, my father came to the class as a surprise to encourage and support me. His intentions were kind, but as an 11-year-old girl, his presence embarrassed me. Standing in front of my peers, my emotions overwhelmed me. I was ashamed that I was adopted but I felt guilty that it mattered to me. Why all of sudden did I feel like I was missing something? My adoptive parents had always treated me like their own daughter. I felt as though I was betraying them.

Throughout my teenage years, there were many times when being adopted left me with a myriad of questions and feelings of insecurity. All teenagers struggle with identity issues, but mine were unique to adoptees. I felt adrift, without biology anchoring me.

My mother was extremely supportive of my extracurricular activities, including driving me to dance practice four nights a week. But as I developed, our relationship became increasingly strained. She often accused me of being promiscuous. She would go through my trash can searching for feminine products, and if she didn't find any, she would accuse me of being pregnant. I was always small in stature but anytime that my weight fluctuated, she made snide and insensitive comments. I knew even as a child that I was not her first choice. One night during a terrible argument, she vehemently yelled at me, "I wish we had never adopted you! You were a mistake, and you have ruined my life." Those words devastated and haunted me.

My mother frequently accused my dad and me of conspiring against her. Looking back now, I see that she was jealous of the close bond between us. My parents' marriage was never all that great either. They fought constantly, and my mother made bitterly hurtful comments. My dad has a degenerative disease of his cornea, and his eyesight has been diminishing since his late teens. One night during an argument, my mother called my father "a blind useless bastard." This phrase became a constant refrain during their arguments. It broke my heart listening to the cruelty hurled at my father. When I asked him to help me understand why my mother was so mean and hurtful, he gently explained that she had her own insecurities. Apparently, she had never been an outwardly affectionate person. He assured me that my mother loved me deeply. Not until I was an adult, however, did I realize that my father was right.

Teenage girls and their mothers typically fight, but I felt our relationship was unusually complicated. As I matured, I learned her life was not easy and began to understand her much better. She had experienced profound heartache, suffering several miscarriages, and giving birth to a stillborn girl. Additionally, she was the only driver in the household until I was old enough to get my driver's license. I am sure that, at times, this was a burdensome responsibility. On top of this, there were many other tasks she had to perform herself because of my dad's poor vision.

As a young woman, however, my emotions overwhelmed rational thought. I felt rejected. Not just rejected once but rejected twice: first by my birth mother and later by my adoptive mother. Why did neither of them want me or love me? Who would literally throw their baby away like trash? What was wrong with me? When I become a mother, will I reject my child too?

The truth is, I vacillated between guilt over betraying my adoptive parents (by wondering about my "real parents") and genuine appreciation of the life I led. Overall, I truly had a wonderful childhood. One might even say that it was the storybook tale of a privileged, well-loved child. I was a dancer and a cheerleader in middle school and high school. I was blessed with many friends and a close circle of best friends. I had boyfriends.

Perhaps most importantly, to this day, both of my parents are always there when I need them. Their love for me is unconditional, and they lovingly support me, no matter what situation I face.

After I turned fifteen, I had one of many health scares. I had always experienced complications with my menstrual cycle, including an extremely heavy flow lasting up to nine days, horrible cramps, severe headaches, nausea, and dizziness. My mom had taken me to a gynecologist, Dr. Miller, soon after I began menstruating. But at age fifteen, the symptoms were worsening, and she took me for another exam. The doctor prescribed birth control pills to alleviate the pain and heavy flow. Soon after that, the doctor's office called to request a follow-up appointment. Dr. Miller kindly explained that my Pap smear results showed some abnormal cells and asked my mother for permission to perform a biopsy.

The cells were indeed precancerous and required surgery. I did not know at the time that this would be the first of many surgeries. I was terrified. I had never been under anesthesia, and quite frankly, I had never heard of a girl having surgery on her private parts. One night before the surgery, I overheard my parents talking. My mother said, "James, I hope this surgery is not a sign of what's in store for us. We do not know what medical problems run in her biological family. We have to be prepared for whatever may come." This frightened me terribly.

Once again, remarks that referred to my adoption and all that was unknown about me left me feeling extremely insecure. However, this particular time, I also became enraged. How could my biological mother not know that my new family would need information regarding family medical history? How could she not care enough to keep me healthy and safe?

Growing up and becoming a teenager is hard enough without constantly feeling burdened by rejection, abandonment, and uncertainty. I struggled throughout most of my teenage years with these emotions and the additional guilt that somehow, I was disloyal to my adoptive family. There were too many moments when someone unwittingly would make a comment that reminded me that I was adopted. I did not really know who I was. I never really talked much about this turmoil with my family or friends, and I most definitely did not speak of my innermost feelings. Being adopted and all the attendant emotions were sensitivities that I kept to myself and dealt with in my own way.

I always knew that when I became of age, I would request my original birth records and look for the answers to all the questions that had haunted me throughout my young life.

****

Monday, March 31, 1998. It was one week before my eighteenth birthday. My anticipation grew to the point that every nerve fiber in my body was vibrating. I would be eligible very soon to request a copy of my birth certificate and all my records! I had to contain my excitement because I purposely had not told anyone what I was doing. Later, I shared the information with my father, but for now, this was my private, personal quest to solve the mystery that had preoccupied me for a very long time. I would finally know who I am. It had to be the longest week of my life. As soon as I woke up on my birthday, I called the Department of Social Services in Atlanta, Georgia. I timidly asked the receptionist, Mary, how to obtain my original birth paperwork. I felt embarrassed, although I knew such an inquiry was routine for her. I imagined she was thinking, "poor girl, I hope she's not disappointed." In reality, Mary was lovely and patiently guided me through the process, outlining what I would need to gain access and copies of my records.

Finally, I would learn more about myself and meet my birth mother.

For the next four days, I raced to check my mail. On the sixth day, my heart fluttered when I read the return address: Department of Social Services. I immediately started filling out the requisite paperwork. It took me a little over two hours to complete the documents and carefully seal and stamp the envelope that held so much promise. That night, I drove to the closest post office to drop off the bulky package. I did not want to risk putting it in my mailbox. I wanted to make sure that the key to my identify shipped the very next day.

It was a mild relief to have completed the first step. However, as the unknown still loomed and the promise of resolution came closer, the actual waiting began. Mary had told me that it could take up to six weeks for my original birth records to arrive. I did not know how I could ever wait that long. During the next five weeks and four days, I was not myself. Yes, I went about my daily life – working at a neonatal clinic, studying to become a nurse, and lounging at home at night. But I did not go out with friends or co-workers as usual. My mind was consumed with fear, happiness, guilt, and impatience. My family, friends, and co-workers commented on my changed behavior, but I just said I wasn't feeling well. I was not ready to tell anyone – including my adoptive parents – what I was doing or explain my reasons for searching for my birth family.

Friday, May 15, 1998. I had a gut feeling the paperwork would arrive today. I was correct. When I came home from work for an early lunch, a thick manila envelope boldly labeled "Department of Social Services" was waiting in my mailbox. Again, with a pounding heart, I took the envelope upstairs to my second-floor apartment. I knew at that moment that I would not return to work that day. I needed to be alone. I understood that envelope's contents were going to bring to the surface all of the conflicts that I had felt over the years about my adoption. My employer was not surprised when I called saying I was not feeling well enough to come back to work because I had not been myself because for the past several weeks. I sat on my bed holding the envelope as tears streamed down my face and soaked the pages. My entire body was shaking. I finally had - in my hands - what I had spent eighteen years of my life wondering about. Who am I? Where did I come from? Who are my parents? Do they ever think about me? I truly believed that this envelope held the answers to a multitude of questions. It would reveal my life story.

I could not have been more disappointed. Pages and pages of blank hospital documents emerged, yielding few answers. **"Abandoned, info unknown"** was written in bold black letters across the records. There were a few crumbs of information about my five-week stay in the neonatal unit at the Tri-County Medical Center, and I gorged on those tiny morsels. I learned that I was four to six weeks premature. There was data that recorded my birth weight and growth. That I was a breech birth. That my lungs were progressing. That I required an apnea monitor. That the medical staff had named me Baby Mary. That I was likely bi-racial because I was born with Mongolian spots, congenital birthmarks usually found in individuals of Black or Asian ethnicity. That strange detail was the most surprising.

The enclosed police report was equally uninformative. Privacy laws require that identifying information remains private. But the report did include the following:

> Upon arriving at the scene, newborn baby was found wrapped in a towel. The newborn was still bloody with the umbilical cord still intact. Umbilical cord tied off unprofessionally. Newborn female having difficulty breathing, will be transported to Tri-County Medical Center. She is in protective custody.

This was all a total shock. Patricia and James had told me that I had been abandoned and that they had adopted me after living 7-1/2 months with a foster family. Apparently, my parents had truly shared all that they knew with me, which was very little. Not even Social Services felt it was important enough to share with my parents that my birth was premature and that my health had been precarious.

Again, I was flooded with anger. Why does an abandoned child have no rights? Why must identifying information stay hidden from her? But those painful thoughts were overshadowed by another set of questions and another kind of rage. Why did my birth mother dispose of me as quickly as she could? Why was I discarded like trash? How could my biological mother not even clean me off? Why didn't she leave me at a fire station or somewhere I would be safely found?

My heart shattered. My birth mother did not care about me at all. I was utterly unwanted. I had imagined that she was probably very young. That she did not want to raise a baby or did not know how. I never imagined that she was selfish and careless. My fantasies that *she* was looking for *me* quickly evaporated. I had registered at many adoption reunion registries, but clearly my biological mother had not.

After reading the hospital records and the police report, I turned to the two enclosed local newspaper articles. Both blared the identical headline: **Newborn Baby Girl Abandoned**. One was dated April 1, 1980, the day after I was found. It reported scant details of the abandonment and a request for anyone with information to contact the police department. The second article was published several days later, indicating that the police were still searching for a link as to the identity of the abandoned newborn. It also reiterated the police report, saying that I was taken to Tri-County Medical Center's neonatal intensive care unit. The police and newspaper reports differed in their assessment of my condition; the former labeled me unstable, whereas the newspaper described me in stable condition.

Not one piece of paper in the long-awaited packet gave the slightest clue as to my identity. The only helpful detail was the location of my birth: Savannah, Georgia. At this point, my face was splotchy, and my eyes were burning, rendering me unable to read further. I was beyond exhausted and succumbed to a short, fitful nap. My dreams were chaotic, and the feeling that I was falling kept awakening me. I have since read this nightmare is common and may represent the individual's sense or inadequacy or fear of being out of control. Both interpretations certainly described me.

****

I decided to plough ahead and read the rest of the contents of the Department of Social Services package. Maybe there was a seed of information yet to spring forth. Based on what I had read so far, I did not expect anything as encouraging as what I read next. There was a hand-written letter from a doctor and his wife, a nurse, from the hospital where I had spent the first five weeks of my life:

If there is any problem in finding Baby Mary a home, let me say that my wife and I would graciously and lovingly accept her into our home permanently. We both love her and desire the best for her.

We would appreciate it if you would take action one way or the other. We feel that she needs to be in her permanent home very soon now. She already has a close bond and attachment for first, my wife, and second, for me.

We feel that if she needs to readjust to a new environment, it would be beneficial for her to make the change now. However, we wish her to remain with us until she finds a permanent home. Please contact us if there is any way that she could become our child.

Of course, the doctor's name was blacked out. But for now that did not matter. Here were two people who loved me and wanted me!

The next set of correspondence was between an adoption agency and my adoptive parents:

Dear Mr. and Mrs. Peters: We are writing to inform you that we have found a newborn baby girl that is waiting to be adopted. She is seven months old and declared medically

healthy. We did want to inform you that we
cannot rule out the possibility that she is bi-
racial ...

The letter went on to explain about my Mongolian spots,

my olive complexion, and other signs indicating my ethnic

background was unclear. My adoptive mother Patricia

wrote back to the case worker:

My husband and I are so extremely excited to
hear that you have a baby girl ready for us to
adopt. We have waited so long for this little
girl. We do not care what color she is, or if
she is bi-racial. We cannot wait to meet her
and bring her home. We will be naming her
Kate. Her nursery is already set up and there
is a closet full of brand new clothes and toys
galore.

Imagine my elation. Not one loving family who wanted me,

but two! I genuinely felt doubly blessed.

As is customary, the adoption process is lengthy.

At five weeks, I was discharged from the hospital to foster

parents Sharon and Walter Wilson, whose whereabouts and

identities were unknown to me until recently. They had

been contacted by Social Services when I was two weeks old, still in the hospital NICU. As per protocol, Social Services disclosed that I was very premature and may have medical issues and asked if the Wilsons were still willing to foster me. They welcomed me and, as I have later learned, wanted to adopt me too. A triple blessing.

Sharon Wilson had written a background summary for my permanent records, and it was apparent I was lovingly cared for. Of course, I do not remember anything from that time.

> Baby Mary's hair has a reddish tint. Her eyes are blue. Her skin appears to have a slight olive base. She smiles and laughs at us and is good-natured. Mary sleeps through the night. At her last pediatric checkup, she weighed 9 lbs. 4 oz. The doctor recommended that inoculations be delayed until she is an age-appropriate weight. On July 24, 1980, she turned from her stomach to her back unassisted.

Despite these few visible bright spots amid blank records, I finished reading feeling profoundly disappointed. I had anticipated finding clues that would lead to a joyful reunion with my birth mother. I had imagined our first conversation. I had envisioned an affirmation that she, too, wanted me. I had thought that the mystery of my origins would be solved. Instead, I was left feeling even more bereft.

****

After several weeks, my self-pity and sense of defeat subsided enough for me to reread each document again. I read each word, each line, several times. Suddenly, I had a hopeful thought: The Department of Social Services was not allowed to release identifying information, but I was certainly allowed to search further and find it on my own.

This realization propelled me into an action plan, beginning with the local Atlanta, Georgia newspaper articles identifying the Haverhill Police Department. First, I would go to the public library there and read the original articles on microfiche. Second, I would visit the police station where the initial report was filed. That thought led to a third possible step, and I read the incident report more closely. It listed the address of the house where I was found *and* the name of the person who reportedly found me! I could tell that this information was supposed to be expunged, so a careless mistake became my lucky break. I would visit the house.

The following weekend, my close friend Barbara and I sped to Atlanta from my apartment in LaGrange, Georgia. We spent the entire day at the library poring over microfilmed newspaper articles and eventually located the originals. As I had hoped, they revealed more significant details, including the names of the police officer and the social worker who were on the scene that night in 1980.

Determined, we drove to the Haverhill Police Station next, and Barbara insisted that she accompany me inside for moral support. I had not thought about what I would say or even ask, but adrenaline and curiosity overtook me. When an officer greeted us, I blurted out, "Hi, I was wondering if there is anyone here who was also working in 1980?" The officer appeared confused but asked me to wait a moment and then disappeared.

He returned with an imposing older gentleman, who asked me to follow him. Sitting in the Police Captain's office, I was sweating and shaking as if I were in trouble.

I cleared my throat and bluntly got to the point, "Captain, thank you for taking the time to speak with me. I am here looking for my birth family." He stared straight at me, and I froze. I paused and waited seemingly forever for his response. This literally felt like the moment of truth.

Captain Rodgers began softly, "It can't be you. You just can't be that newborn baby girl." I swallowed, speechless. He leaned across his desk and gently took my hand.

"Is your birthday March 31, 1980?"

"Yes, sir, it is."

He stood up with tears in his eyes, walked slowly around the desk, and hugged me.

"I was there that cold, windy night. I worked your case. It was so chilly that night, and you were so tiny. You weren't even cleaned up. When we arrived at the scene, you were wrapped in a bloody towel lying on a paper bag, and your skin was cold to the touch. Your breaths were shallow, your lips were blue. The paramedics were utterly silent as they moved around, doing everything possible to save you. We knew that you had to be taken to a hospital immediately to have any chance of survival. I only got a brief glance at you before you were taken away.

I worked the scene the whole night, interviewing residents and canvassing the surrounding neighbors. It was a daunting task. We spent days looking for answers, for any possible clue as to who had left you. We told all the area hospitals to notify us if any female came in who had recently delivered, miscarried, or showed signs of recent pregnancy. After several days passed, we knew that our window had closed. There was very little hope of locating the person responsible for abandoning you.

Your story is one that those of us who were there have never forgotten. It is not every day that you receive a call to pick up a newborn girl left out in the cold. None of us – the paramedics nor the police – were ever told how things turned out for you or if you had even survived. You, my sweet girl, have always stayed on my mind."

Captain Rodgers gave me his card and asked me to promise that we would meet again if I were ever back in town. His parting words were, "I am just in awe."

Awe did not begin to describe how I was feeling. Here was a person who knew my story. Someone who met me when I was only hours old. Someone who was instrumental in saving my life. Someone who cared about me. As I hugged him goodbye, my gratitude was overwhelming.

The second my friend Barbara and I exited the station, my tears flowed uncontrollably. The thanks I proffered to Captain Rodgers, however sincere, seemed inadequate. There was no way he could fully understand what our conversation meant to me. Barbara wisely suggested that we stay overnight at a Hampton Inn instead of driving back to LaGrange. Also, one more stop on this trip was absolutely necessary: I had to see the front lawn of the house where I was discarded and abandoned.

That evening, I shared my conviction with Barbara, "My mother is nearby. I am certain about that." She supported me, "If you feel her presence, Kate, you must be right. There is no stronger bond than that of a mother and her daughter." Once again, on my journey of discovery, I felt optimistic.

When we arrived at the address listed on the police incident report, I remained paralyzed in the car. I was hyperventilating as I stared at the front porch steps where I was found. The sight mesmerized me. When I finally got up the courage to ring the doorbell, a pleasant-looking older lady quickly responded, "Yes, may I help you?" I introduced myself and told her the reason for my visit. She was visibly

taken aback but hospitable and introduced herself as
Maxine Gibson.

My expectations were heightened as she cordially
invited us inside. Maxine informed me that her daughter,
Adele, had found me. She further explained that Adele was
a grown woman and had moved out of the area. Maxine
briefly recounted the story of the night of my birth and
proceeded to get her daughter's high school yearbooks for
me to peruse. I instinctively felt a connective link, although
there was no indication that Maxine was my biological
grandmother. Nevertheless, this trip had been a successful
step in my path to self-discovery.

****

When I arrived home from Savannah, my mind and
my emotions were churning. I knew that if I continued my
search at this point, I would be unable to regain my

equilibrium. I feared getting into a pattern of sleeplessness, anxiety, and debilitating depression. So I put all the documents in a drawer and filed their contents in the back of my mind.

For the next eighteen months, I devoted my efforts to my future. I enthusiastically enrolled in nursing school full-time and worked the second shift in a nursing home. I did not have much time for anything else other than an occasional date or outing with friends. During my clinical rotation in school, I was assigned to a neonatal physician, Dr. William Eisner, who became a genuine mentor. He even guided me through the process of sitting for NCLEX, the national state board of nursing. Upon graduation, he hired me full-time.

The only downside was that Dr. Eisner's practice specialized in follow-up care for premature babies. As I listened daily to new mothers swooning and cooing over their newborns, I was constantly reminded of my biological mother's heartlessness. Comments like "she looks just like her father" or "he has his grandmother's smile" reminded me of the hole in my heart. Nevertheless, I was pleased with what I had accomplished and enjoyed my parents' pride over my success. I loved my job so much that I believed that I would work with Dr. Eisner until my retirement.

Fate had other plans, and a drunk driver derailed my future. On the way home from work after just a few months, I was hit dead-on by a drunk driver. It was a horrific car wreck, and I was transported by ambulance to the nearest hospital. After multiple X-rays, MRIs, poking, and prodding, the extent of my injuries was determined: bruised ribs, spit-open lip, black eye, and severe facial burns from the airbag deployment. Worst of all, I suffered multiple broken ankle and foot bones. My parents had frantically arrived at the E.R. and did not leave my side. The orthopedic surgeon vividly compared my shattered bones to a large piece of glass smashed onto concrete. The required reconstructive surgery involved placing a steel rod and plate in my leg with multiple pins and screws. Afterward, I would need intensive physical therapy to regain ankle strength and mobility.

As if this were not upsetting enough, there was even more devasting news: I might never walk again. Even a rigorous therapy regimen did not guarantee that I would recover and become fully mobile. At the very least, I would require an assistive device. At best, I would forever have a distinct limp.

I was twenty-one years old, embarking on a new career, and living independently. That life shattered along with my foot. I was now totally dependent. I had to relinquish my job and apartment to go live with my parents. I could not complete the simplest tasks on my own. I required assistance showering, changing clothes, even navigating around the house. And the ultimate means of independence was stripped from me – I could not drive. My nursing career evaporated too. Even if I could relearn how to walk, I would never again be able to spend my days on my feet rushing around.

Not surprisingly, I became severely depressed, so I began counseling. I spent an average of eight hours a week seeing medical professionals. My schedule included two-hour physical therapy sessions three times a week and one-hour mental health therapy sessions two times a week. This routine went on for eight very slow months. My days were long and tedious. When my parents were at work, the only activity I could manage was watching television. Further, as any grown child who returns to live with her parents knows, it is a difficult adjustment for everyone involved. The only small pleasure I enjoyed was spending evenings talking with my dad.

Although physical therapy was helpful, I was discouraged by my slow progress. After weeks of dependence and inactivity, I finally decided it was time to take control of my life. I announced to my father, "I *will* walk again. And I *will* walk normally." I had formulated a plan to return to school to study education and teach small children. With my associate degree in nursing, I had already completed many required core courses. After much research with my father, I discovered an online program at Pace University. I set goals that I was determined to achieve: to walk normally, complete a bachelor's degree, move back into my own apartment, and get a meaningful job. I would move on with my life – literally and figuratively.

Two years later, contrary to predictions, my gait was completely normal. So was my life. I worked as an assistant teacher at an elementary school, lived independently in an apartment, and socialized again. One night a friend introduced me to one of her boyfriend's close friends, Gregory, a handsome Marine. His blond hair and blue eyes were a striking contrast with his dark olive complexion. His time in the service required grueling workouts, and the results were evident in his trim, muscular physique. Gregory was not actively deployed but was working as an air traffic control tower specialist in the Marines.

Our relationship moved forward quickly, and we had several conversations about the possibility of getting married. However, instead of a marriage proposal, Gregory surprised me with an invitation to pick up and move with him to West Palm Beach, Florida. I was excited at the prospect but reluctant to move so far away from my father. Also, I had a nagging recollection of him saying that he was not sure that Gregory was the right man for me. But dad had also told me that he trusted my ability to decide what was best for me. I decided that going to Florida with Gregory was the right move. Next steps: an apartment for us and a job for me.

Fortunately, my nursing licenses were up-to-date, and I got a perfect job working at a cardiology practice. An office setting was preferable over a hospital since I would not have to spend an entire day on my feet. The nine-to-five daytime hours were desirable too. I was truly independent and very happy. Days at work, nights with Gregory, and weekends at the beach. No kids, little responsibility, and no one to answer to.

****

It happened gradually. Gregory and I were spending less and less time together. He was working later and later. I missed my family and friends and had not met anyone outside of the doctor's office, so I had no one to confide in. When I shared my discontent with Gregory, he dismissed it, saying I would soon adjust to my new circumstances. But I became more and more depressed, and Gregory became increasingly distant. Sometimes he seemed unaware of his surroundings, as if he were in a dream state. Finally, I figured out that Gregory was drinking. But I did not realize the extent of his addiction to alcohol and drugs too.

I began to question my decision to relocate to Florida with Gregory. Did I make a huge mistake? Was my father right about Gregory?

There was one decision that was not debatable: whether to see a gynecologist. With a history of precancerous cervical cells, I needed to have regular check-ups and Pap smears. It was not really a choice. However, the idea of seeing a new gynecologist was fraught with emotional baggage. Since I had had gynecological surgery at age fifteen, I was afraid a new doctor would find another problem. Further, I had seen the same doctors all my life in LaGrange, Georgia, and was accustomed to them. Perhaps worst of all, the upset of not knowing my biological medical history resurfaced.

I carefully researched nearby doctors' credentials and, with trepidation, scheduled an appointment. At the outset of our relationship, like most new couples, Gregory and I discussed our hopes and fears. I had expressed my deep-rooted anxiety about not being able to bear my own children. Although I was blessed with incredibly kind and loving adoptive parents, I nevertheless still struggled with the insecurity of not fully knowing who I was. I wanted to provide my children with the answers to questions about their identity that I never had. My intention was to have a biological child and then adopt others.

I expected Gregory to understand my fears and my reluctance to go to the gynecologist. He coldly dismissed my concerns saying, "don't be ridiculous. You'll be fine." This conversation precipitated our first major argument, and Gregory stormed out of our apartment. I lay in bed, sobbing and homesick. My instinct was to reach out to my father; I knew he would reassure me. However, pride and stubbornness prevented me from calling. I remembered my father voicing doubts about Gregory earlier and did not want to worry or disappoint him. After all, I was a 22-year-old adult and on my own.

After our argument, Gregory did not return to our apartment until the following morning. He reeked of alcohol. It took a lot of effort to regain my composure, and I went alone to my new gynecologist, Dr. Green. Gregory had not even offered to accompany me. Of course, I had to wait an excruciatingly long time to learn the exam results. When I received the phone call to return to the doctor's office for a follow-up visit, I knew. I positively knew that she would tell me she found more precancerous cells.

So when I was ushered into the doctor's office instead of an exam room, I expected the bad news that came next, "Ms. Peters, there is an indication of cervical cancer." This was even worse news than I envisioned: not precancer – it was cancer.

The next step was a biopsy. Dr. Green described the possible scenarios, including the chance the initial Pap smear results were not accurate. But if they were, based on my medical history, I would require another surgery to scrape the lining of my cervix. My mind was racing with a jumble of unpleasant thoughts. What if there was cancer that had spread? How could I undergo major surgery with my parents living fourteen hours away? What if Gregory continued to drink and act indifferent to my concerns? And the most troubling question of all was, what if I were unable to have biological children?

Fortunately, Dr. Green was able to perform the biopsy that day in her office. That was the easy part. Now I had to wait at least two weeks for what I feared would be more bad news. I left the doctor's office in a fog of upset and made two phone calls: the first to notify work that I was taking off the rest of the day, and the second to Gregory to please meet me at home right away.

I was pleasantly surprised when Gregory came home and held me while I wept. He promised to be with me when the biopsy results came in. It was torturous waiting, and I was so worried that I began to have debilitating headaches and could not eat. Despite Gregory's improved attitude, I had never felt so alone. I still had not discussed my health with my parents. When the phone rang a few days later, the caller ID showed Dr. Green's number. Timidly, I answered. The voice was hers, not a nurse's, so I knew the news would be bad. She asked me to come to the office right away to discuss the dreaded biopsy results. Gregory agreed to meet me there, and he held my hand, repeating reassurances.

Dr. Green explained that the cancer was completely curable and had not spread. She described a simple outpatient procedure to remove the diseased cells and assured me the prognosis was excellent. Further, she said that I should plan to have Pap smears twice a year as a preventative measure. We scheduled the surgery for the following week.

The nerve-racking night before the operation, I waited for Gregory to come home. As the clock ticked slowly, I waited and waited. Of course, I became increasingly upset, anxious, and angry. Maybe he just went out with friends after work, but why didn't he bother to call? I took a Tylenol PM to get a good night's sleep, figuring Gregory would be home late and accompany me to the hospital in the morning.

I was wrong and awoke to an empty apartment. It was evident that he had not come home at all that night. I was beyond furious, but I was certain about one decision. I was finished with our relationship. Once I recovered from the surgery, I vowed to leave Gregory and go home to LaGrange.

At this moment, I did not have time to be mired in anger at Gregory nor to thoroughly plan my next steps. I needed to find someone to drive me to and from the hospital. A co-worker, Jessie, and I had become friendly, so I called her at 6:00 a.m. and explained my situation. She readily agreed and even said she would not leave me alone;

she would stay with me. During the car ride with Jessie, I vented about Gregory, sharing my suspicions about his alcohol use – or worse – and his inattentiveness. She was caring and comforting, and I knew we would stay in touch after I moved back home.

****

According to Dr. Green, the procedure went very well. But the following scene at my apartment did not. Gregory sat on the couch, completely hungover and started to yell at me, "Where have you been? I called you at work and they said you were out of the office today. And you haven't answered my calls."

"You are a complete jerk," I screamed. "I have been at the hospital all day having surgery! You were supposed to drive me there and stay with me! You are my boyfriend and you abandoned me and got drunk!"

I threw my sweater at him and continued my rant, "I hate you! As soon as I've healed from surgery, I am packing my things! I am going home where my family treats me the way I deserve, you ..." I slammed the door to my bedroom and collapsed onto the bed. The next six weeks were predictably miserable. Gregory and I fought viciously and constantly. I could not even bear being in the same room with him.

Our discord hung in the air like a threatening storm cloud. Finally, I made the inevitable phone call. "Daddy," I said softly, "I want to come home." He replied instantly, "Oh, baby, just let me know when you are leaving. Your mother and I will get everything ready for you." I still had not told them about my surgery. That conversation could wait. My father's welcoming reaction to my move home was totally characteristic of him. There was no "you need to stick it out." There was no "I told you so." Instead, there was unconditional love and acceptance.

I did not wait to give notice at work. I was finished with Gregory and finished with Florida and planned to leave Saturday morning. On Friday, my dad called to say they had rented me a one-bedroom apartment near them in LaGrange, and that they would have groceries and other necessities there when I arrived.

I had the presence of mind to go to my apartment's leasing office and explained that I had a family emergency back home. I informed the office that the other occupant would not be leaving, and they agreed to take my name off the lease. Relief flooded me because I did not want to ruin my good credit by terminating the lease early. Now, the apartment was Gregory's sole responsibility.

Friday night, I completed my departure preparations. As usual, Gregory was not yet home, which was perfectly fine with me. In the span of just a few hours, I had rented a U-Haul truck, packed my belongings, and loaded the car. Fortunately, my neighbors were two young men who graciously loaded the heavy household items into the U-Haul. Most of the apartment's contents were mine, so my new home would be well-furnished.

I drove non-stop from West Palm Beach to LaGrange and the radio blared with music that I now associate with freedom. My relief was palpable – a heavy weight of unhappiness had lifted – and I knew I had made a wise decision. When I saw the highway exit leading to my hometown, I exhaled deeply and audibly. I pulled into my new apartment complex, and there, waiting in the parking lot, were my parents. Immediately, I jumped into my father's arms and was welcomed by his warm, wraparound hug. My parents helped me move my belongings, and I stayed up late unpacking. By morning, the apartment looked as if I had always lived there.

I had not slept for twenty-four hours and crashed into bed for the deepest, most peaceful sleep I experienced in a very long time. When I awoke, my phone indicated fourteen missed calls. I had turned it off so as not to deal with Gregory, but I knew that the messages were from him. I ignored them and spent a very pleasant day catching up with my parents. When they left, I enjoyed a saccharine Lifetime Channel movie in my pajamas.

The telephone's insistent ringing interrupted my tranquil mood because of course, I knew it would be Gregory. I had to deal with him eventually and now felt strong enough to answer the call. Unsurprisingly, the conversation was argumentative. Gregory denied partying or drinking or drugging and claimed no responsibility for the state of our relationship. As the call wound down, Gregory said he was coming to LaGrange, and that was that. He hung up as I was still protesting. I believed he would indeed show up, but I put his return out of my mind and continued to move forward, getting my life back on track.

Luckily, my previous employer, an elementary school, welcomed me back as an assistant teacher, and I started working the following week. I only needed a few more hours of classroom experience before taking the PACE certification exam and becoming a lead teacher. My life had a calmness and a direction that had been absent for a long time.

****

When Gregory arrived in LaGrange, he bombarded me with phone calls begging me to take him back. He promised to be attentive and more sensitive and not to drink. His campaign even entailed asking my mother to exert her influence on me to give him another chance. I am really not sure why, but I eventually caved. Our relationship was restored to the positive patterns we enjoyed at its beginning: long, intimate phone conversations and enjoyable dates. It felt as if we had never moved to West Palm Beach or had a life fraught with conflict. I was also socializing with friends, enjoying work, and relishing the closeness with my family.

As the time for my six-month gynecological follow-up visit approached, I was not nervous or concerned about seeing Dr. Miller again. Dr. Green in Florida had indicated that the surgery had been successful, and she did not anticipate future issues. At the visit, I did not bother to tell Dr. Miller about this surgery because I had packed Florida away in my mind. I was pleased and relieved to see Dr. Miller again, as I had always felt comfortable with her.

Two weeks after the appointment, I was still waiting for the routine Pap smear results and felt no trepidation. When the phone rang in my classroom, the caller ID alerted me to Dr. Miller, who asked me to come back to her office. I knew that this visit would bring more bad news. Indeed, cancerous cells had invaded my cervix again, so I could no longer withhold the information about my most recent surgery from her; I authorized the release of my medical records from Florida.

I was not prepared for Dr. Miller's recommendation that I have a hysterectomy to address this third cancer reoccurrence. She explained that it was a significant risk *not* to have surgery because my family's medical history was unknown. I understood that I had to make a life or death decision, one that would dramatically alter my life forever.

Now, the fears and insecurity about being adopted, which had lain dormant for years, overwhelmed me. As I cried in Dr. Miller's office, I managed to choke out how much I wanted to be pregnant and birth a biological child. Taking out my uterus meant taking away this dream. But Dr. Miller stressed that a pregnancy would be extremely risky due to my cervical insufficiency.

That night, I invited my parents to join Gregory and me for dinner. Although I was determined to make my own decision, I needed my support system. My parents were devastated by the news of my previously undisclosed surgery. They were disappointed that they had not been there to take care of me. However, their overriding concern was my health and wellbeing. At the time, I already knew how I would handle this setback, but I did not share my thoughts.

Life resumed a modicum of normalcy, except for the newly increasing anxiety and sadness over the prospect of not having a baby. What did I do to cope? I purposely got pregnant.

Gregory was very excited about the pregnancy, but as my due date neared, our relationship began a familiar downward spiral. He was coming home drunk, and drug paraphernalia now littered the apartment. The decision to leave him again was easy because I now had zero tolerance for his bad behavior. I wanted my daughter to be nurtured in the safe and loving home that I alone could provide. So I broke up with Gregory and braved pregnancy and childbirth alone.

The pregnancy was not easy. In fact, it was terrifying, and I obsessively feared a devastating loss. Since the fetus was not receiving enough nutrients through the twisted umbilical cord, she was not growing properly. This meant that there were serious concerns about the lungs' maturation, so I was hospitalized overnight for steroid injections to improve their function. During the first seven months, I went into early labor three times and was hospitalized to receive fluids intravenously to stop the contractions. The third time was the last because, although my daughter had not turned or dropped in utero yet, the cord was wrapped around her neck. The doctors decided to schedule the delivery at 32 weeks and induce labor.

The delivery itself was fairly easy, but once tiny Pearl Gracie Peters was born on July 16, 2005, I did not see her for an hour because she was blue and not breathing properly. Once she was in my arms like most new mothers, I was immediately enthralled and in love. But I felt that my experience of motherhood was uniquely extraordinary since Pearl's beginning represented the ending of a lifetime of fears.

****

When my precious, long-wished-for Pearl Gracie Peters was a toddler, I worked as a middle school teacher for children with special needs. I bought my own home, a small two-bedroom brick ranch directly across the street from my parents. After a full day at work, I enjoyed a simple routine, playing with Pearl and having dinner with my parents. I took Gregory to court, and he willingly relinquished all paternal rights.

I never regretted splitting up with Gregory and did not miss him at all. But the fact remained, I was lonely. I was not interested in a serious relationship, but I did want companionship. My best friend Julie and I spent a lot of time together, and she encouraged me to join an online dating site. I strongly resisted, citing the dating horror stories I heard. I had always dreamt that I would meet my lifelong partner in a traditional way, like meeting at work or through a mutual friend. But as much as I resisted, Julie persisted until she eventually wore me down. Perhaps I would meet someone I enjoyed talking to or going to a movie. Nothing more than a pleasant, superficial relationship. Being a good mother to Pearl took priority, and she was my world.

Initially, my online dating experiences were exactly as I expected — men looking for hook-ups or posting dishonest profiles. Nevertheless, I still spent some evenings chatting online and even accepted a few dates, all predictably awful. I decided that there were enough enjoyable conversations to merit remaining online to chat but not enough to meet in person on dates.

It took an exceptional man to help me change my mind about dating — Ethan Kendall. The two of us developed an online connection and an attraction, so I was not surprised when he suggested meeting in person. By this point, I was looking forward to getting home at night to chat with him. Ethan was recently divorced, with a son named Christian. He seemed as lonely as I was. Besides my initial reluctance, there was a significant obstacle to overcome; I lived in LaGrange, and he lived about an hour and a half away in Atlanta. Ethan offered to drive to me for our first date, and since I did not think this would be a regular long-distance event, I agreed to get together.

We met for lunch at an Applebee's right off a highway exit, and our conversation flowed easily. Ethan is tall and very slender, with smiling blue-grey eyes, and I was definitely attracted. After lunch, we took a drive through the country and chatted effortlessly. We discussed more than typical first-date topics, sharing details about our children (Christian was just a little older than Pearl), our jobs (Ethan worked in golf course management), our families (he had four siblings), and our hopes and priorities. We were both reluctant for the date to end. The attraction seemed very real.

Evening chats on the telephone replaced our online ones, and we spoke most nights. Ethan was wonderful about driving to see me, and we would happily spend the day together. Although we had not yet met each other's children, we were beginning to discuss the progression of our relationship. Eventually, I introduced him to Pearl and was delighted with how well they interacted. Soon after, I met his son Christian, and we enjoyed the silly movie *Beverly Hills Chihuahua* together.

About a year into our relationship, Ethan and I spent all of our available free time together. It was time to introduce Pearl, who was four years old, and Christian, who was five. Their first meeting exceeded our expectations, as they happily played and shared toys. Soon our dates were double-dates at venues like Chuck E. Cheese, Gattitown

Pizza, and outdoor parks. Our families met too, and it was thrilling to be given the gift of Ethan's parents, siblings, in-laws, nephews, and nieces. After all, I had spent a lot of time and energy unsuccessfully searching for a family — my birth family. Now, I had a new family who accepted and embraced me.

After dating for about two years, Ethan proposed, and I enthusiastically accepted. Like many people who meet online, I never expected to find my forever soulmate through a dating app. But I did. We had a November wedding in LaGrange, and it could not have been a more perfect ceremony and reception. As I got ready that morning, my thoughts surprisingly turned to my biological family. Did my mother ever get married? What would it be like if she attended my wedding? Do I have any stepsiblings?

My adoptive father, who was my real father in every sense, was walking me down the aisle and giving me away. But he was giving me with love to a husband whom he knew cherished me. My father was not throwing me away as my birth mother had done.

It was easy to promise Ethan that we would share all of life's joys and sorrows together forever. To promise him that we were joining not just ourselves together as one, but also joining our two families together as a whole unit.

****

During our engagement, Ethan and I had to confront a significant decision: where would we live? Ethan had been doing the lion's share of the ninety-minute commute between his Atlanta home and mine in LaGrange. Ethan's custody agreement stipulated that his son Christian would live with him every other weekend and twice during the week; it was untenable for him to drive so far so frequently. Additionally, Ethan had worked as a golf course manager for the same company for over fourteen years, and employment opportunities in my small hometown were nonexistent. Settling in Atlanta was obviously the preferable and logical choice.

I was terrified to move away from LaGrange for a variety of reasons. Primarily, I feared a repeat of the consequences of my move to West Palm Beach years ago with Gregory. It felt like an enormous risk for me to give up everything again – parents, job, and friends. Plus, Pearl was thriving in kindergarten, and I was reluctant to transition her to a new school. Ethan did not seem to fully comprehend the enormity of my concerns, and uncharacteristic tension surfaced in our relationship.

I consulted my wise and understanding father about my concerns. He told me that Ethan was the right husband and moving to Atlanta was the right decision. Although my dad reassured me that we would remain in close contact and see each other regularly, I knew he was saddened. This move was more emotionally complicated for him than the one to West Palm Beach. This time, not only would he be far from me, but he would also miss his only granddaughter, Pearl.

A new chapter of my life was beginning, and I recognized that I had always coped remarkably well with changes, both unexpected and planned. So with optimism and resolve, I accompanied Ethan on several trips to Atlanta to find an apartment. We chose a suburb near his job and his son. I had done an extensive job search in the area and secured an office job at an insurance company with excellent pay and benefits. It was not my ideal job because I wanted to remain in education, but the PACE program that enabled me to teach in LaGrange was unavailable in Atlanta. But everything in life has tradeoffs, and this job was a solid compromise.

Ethan and I agreed that I would stay in LaGrange until Pearl finished kindergarten and I completed the school year teaching students with special needs. I thought that Pearl needed this security because she had lived her entire life close to my parents, who provided a lot of her childcare. However, she adjusted better to a new family, new town, and new school than I did.

Although we settled into a pleasant routine in Atlanta and I enjoyed my new job, I initially struggled with all the changes. I continually reminded myself of all I had managed to overcome and of all that I had gained by marrying Ethan. One of the best parts was being welcomed by his large, close family. However, I missed my parents and hometown and became increasingly depressed. Some days, I was so despondent that I barely spoke to Ethan. I think that I unjustly blamed him for my unhappiness. He is good-natured and rarely raises his voice, but I knew that he was frustrated with me. Therapy helped me tremendously when I struggled with my condition after the car accident, and I sought counseling again.

Gradually, my outlook improved. I genuinely enjoyed the time spent together with my new extended family. Ethan had told his siblings about my birth story and adoption, and one night, the subject came up at my in-law's dinner table. They were all very curious and asked if I planned to resume the search for my biological family. I shared the story of my minimal birth records and of the encounters on my trip to Savannah. The conversation was animated, and Ethan's family listened and questioned me in such a way that I felt detached from my story. It seemed like my history was that of a different person. I had never looked at my life from anyone else's perspective. Ethan's family's consensus was that I should continue searching.

****

Although my feelings of incompleteness and insecurity had never fully subsided, my quest for a biological family had been latent for many, many years. If one has not experienced the psychological impact of adoption, it may be hard to comprehend fully that an absence can be an acute presence. But I always felt like a piece of my heart was missing. Ironically, the family I gained through marriage energized me to recommence my search for another family. I felt ready to look, but I was utterly unprepared for the fluctuations of hope, surprise, and disappointment that followed.

I began to systematically study all the birth and incident records that I had tucked away. Unlike previously, I took notes and cataloged the names of the people listed in the reports. I became so engrossed in my research that I was disengaging from Ethan, Pearl, and Christian. My evenings were spent online scouring school yearbooks and contacting people who attended high school in Savannah, Georgia, where I was born. I was convinced that my birth mother must be among them.

A perfect opportunity arose to return to Savannah. My sister-in-law Laurel was planning to visit her daughter Carly, who attended college there. Laurel suggested going together to the house where I was found. So we drove together to Savannah for the dual purpose of researching and visiting. On the road, I hummed with anticipation, and as we got closer, expectation morphed into certainty and connection.

I felt compelled to meet Maxine Gibson again. After all, she met me when I was just minutes old and had even held me. Laurel reluctantly accompanied me as I rang the doorbell, and Maxine answered. I said, "I am not sure if you remember me, but I am the baby you found on your doorstep. I visited you about ten years ago." Then, I introduced Laurel, and Maxine invited us both into her living room. Within seconds, an attractive middle-aged woman entered from the direction of the kitchen, who Maxine introduced as her daughter Adele.

As my stomach flip-flopped and my heart fluttered, Laurel nudged my leg. I knew – without a shred of doubt – that Adele, standing in front of me, was my biological mother. Maxine introduced me, "Adele, this is the baby that I found many years ago on our front lawn."

"But, mom, don't you remember?" interrupted Adele. "*I* found the baby and called you to come home from work. I was napping after school and awoke to check the mail. That's when I found her."

The oddness of this exchange was striking. Something did not seem quite right. Regardless, Adele asked me questions about my life, and I quickly got to the point. "Can you remember anyone in your high school who was pregnant around the time that I was found?"

I knew that the answer was directly in front of me. But Adele continued, "No, I can't recall anyone, but you look Italian. There were many exchange students at my school, so maybe it was one of them." There was a brief silence, broken by Adele blurting, "You couldn't possibly be part of this family. We all have blonde hair and green eyes. And you really do look Italian." I refrained from saying that her hair was not blonde, it was dyed, but I did retort, "I actually do have green eyes."

Our conversation did not progress in the way I had hoped, but I had an inspired idea. I asked if Adele and Maxine would be willing to take a photo with me. Not only did I want a keepsake of people who had seen me as a premature newborn, but I also planned to analyze the picture for clues to my identity. The visit ended cordially, with my agreeing to send a copy of the photo, and we exchanged phone numbers.

As soon as Laurel and I got into the car, she said, "Holy crap, that is your mother!" My thoughts and heart were racing with questions: Why didn't Adele acknowledge me as her child? Was my birth a secret that she never disclosed to her mother? Will she contact me later, in private? Why was it meaningful to her to have my picture? I quickly texted her the photo, hoping she would be encouraged to talk to me. I received a simple "thank you" in reply.

****

When I came home to Atlanta, the excitement of my discoveries in Savannah propelled me to talk nonstop to Ethan about the trip. He was skeptical about my assertion that Adele was my mother and professed not to see any resemblance between us in the photo. Although Ethan is extraordinarily kind, he is also somewhat opinionated and judgmental. I did not let his disbelief dampen my spirits nor dissuade me from investigating further. I *knew* – without a doubt – that Adele was my mother.

As I processed my conversation with the Gibson's, I recalled another peculiar comment. When asked who she thought might have left me on their lawn, Adele stated, "I don't know anyone who would just leave their baby on a doorstep. But I do remember that around the same time, someone left litters of kittens on our yard." What? She was comparing me to a litter of kittens?

My sister-in-law Laurel and I frequently spoke about our trip and resolved to return to Savannah very soon. I texted Adele, letting her know of an upcoming visit, and we arranged to have dinner together. I was elated about the prospect; I was positive that – without Maxine present — Adele would confess the circumstances of my birth.

I also contacted Lydia Summers, the investigative child services detective on the scene on that front lawn forty years ago, and we planned to meet. Additionally, I reached out to the two paramedics who were present, Bob O'Connor and Timothy Bryant, and they agreed to join us for lunch. The trip was all set, and the truth was within reach!

The night before Laurel and I were leaving, I received a terse, disappointing text from Adele, "I forgot that I have a prior engagement and can't meet." My instincts told me that she was pushing me away and had no intention of ever communicating with me again. I felt an all too familiar sense of rejection.

Lydia, Bob, and Timothy arrived promptly to our lunch at Ruby Tuesdays. We were all on edge. No one ordered food, just coffee. None of us had met previously; our only contact was by phone. However, it did not take long for everyone to become comfortable, and the three of them each emphatically depicted the drama of March 31, 1980. The lunch meeting was exceedingly productive because each professional detailed their view of my story. They described the shock of seeing my imperiled condition. As they waited for the rescue ambulance, Lydia, Bob, and Timothy all believed that whoever left me should have at least sought medical attention. My life had hung in the balance. As the team sped to the Tri-County Medical Center, Bob cradled me in the backseat of his emergency vehicle.

I described to the group my encounter with Adele Gibson and shared my conviction that she was my mother. Lydia confirmed that she, too, had suspected Adele.

However, since she was underage at the time and showed no physical signs of recent pregnancy, the authorities were not permitted to question her. The four of us chatted for several very emotional hours, and Lydia, Bob, and Timothy expressed their amazement and pleasure that I had located them. They echoed Captain Rodgers's words that my case was literally unforgettable. It is not every day, they agreed, that you find a newborn on the brink of death and later have the opportunity to build an adult friendship. We were linked by a unique connection and exchanged contact information. Before parting, I asked if they would take a picture with me. I still treasure this photo of the people who saved my life.

Upon returning home, I spent hours gathering more information about Adele's life and family. She appeared to be a very private person, without an online presence. I had extended her a Facebook friend request soon after I had met her. To this day, the invitation has been ignored. Whenever I planned a trip to Savannah, I texted her with the hope of meeting again. Adele's response was consistent, "I'm sorry, but unfortunately, I am not available." Each text elicited a painful pang of rejection.

Not only was I hurt by Adele's behavior, but I also was puzzled. Why did she not want to at least talk with me, if not sustain a relationship? How could she not feel a need to explain herself? Why did she not want to discuss her experiences or point of view? How could she be devoid of any maternal twinges? All the strangers who subsequently met me – the police officers, social workers, EMTs – had all embraced me. Why not my own mother?

This emotional abandonment, which followed a physical one, seemed somewhat unusual. I had registered on several adoption websites and read countless stories of joyful reunions. Why couldn't I have my own heartwarming story?

****

Eventually, the roller-coaster pattern of obsession, hope, and disappointment plateaued. I was no longer compulsively consumed by my search efforts. Instead, I experienced a modicum of peace and satisfaction with what I had discovered thus far. So once again, my life regained some normalcy. Nights on the computer were eclipsed by my family's busy schedules. Pearl was very involved in gymnastics and competitive cheerleading. Christian was a typical rambunctious boy interested in video games and his peers. And Ethan worked hard at his managerial job and worked out diligently at a gym. I was employed full-time, maintained the household, socialized with friends and family, chauffeured the kids, and helped with homework. We were a typical southern, suburban family of four.

Several months after my trip to Savannah, a text from Ethan while I was at work pivoted my attention. He had read a newspaper article about a girl who located her birth mother using the genealogy website ancestry.com. With his family's encouragement, Ethan had become increasingly supportive of my search and suggested I try the site. He reignited my motivation to obtain more family information. So, of course, I immediately went online and requested a DNA test kit. One hundred dollars was a small price to pay for invaluable data. I sent my saliva swab for analysis, and as I had done at eighteen years old, I waited … and waited … for six long weeks.

I vividly remember the day the email arrived from ancestry.com. A simple link would unlock the mystery of my origins. I was most anxious to get information about my ethnicity because I always struggled with not knowing that basic fact, especially when asked about my olive complexion. Saying "I don't know" left me untethered. Finally, I had the precise answer: 99% European, broken down into 38% Scandinavian, 26% Southern European, and 17% Italian. Aha! The results explained my skin tone and prominent features.

Ancestry.com also reported the identity of possible DNA matches so I could find names along with numbers. The most frequently appearing surname was "Gibson," which is the same as Maxine and Adele's. This came as no surprise. The Gibson's and I matched 689 centimorgans, units of genetic measurement that calculate the distance between two chromosomes. A centimorgan range of 575 to 1330 could mean that the DNA match is a first cousin, half aunt, or possibly a grandparent. There was another name that frequently appeared: Collins. I had a lot of research ahead of me.

If only I could have accessed ancestry.com for my sixth-grade assignment of diagramming a family tree because the site enables people to build a genealogical chart. Although some users post their trees publicly, there is one shortcoming. If someone on the chart is living, their name is blocked out as private. However, I found a way to circumvent this restriction. Ancestry.com allows its users to send a message directly to the tree's "owner."

With much anticipation, I messaged Betty Schmidt, who had shared her tree – our tree – publicly. I explained that we were a very close DNA match and that I would love to talk. My sincere hope was that she would lead me to Adele Gibson. I did not disclose my last name to Betty out of respect (or maybe fear) that word would get back to the Gibson family. When Betty finally responded, we learned that we did not have a direct connection. However, she was a distant cousin on Adele's father's side. I was getting closer and closer to the truth. At the same time, however, I was moving further and further away from Ethan, Pearl, and Christian. Compulsive research supplanted my responsibilities as a wife and mother – yet again.

My resources up until now – birth records, incident reports, letters, witnesses, and DNA matches – all led to one prime suspect: Adele. So it was time to dig further into her life.

I had an unexplored resource available, social media, so Facebook was the next logical step. Using the name Mary Doe, which was how I was identified at birth, I created a fake Facebook profile page. On some level, I knew what I was doing was wrong. If Adele were indeed my mother, I would publicly expose her story and thus, violate her privacy. My actions, if not my intent, were selfish. I did not want to cause Adele or her family pain or embarrassment, but my anger at being lied to fueled me. I posted a request for information about my biological family on Facebook and uploaded relevant newspaper articles and parts of my birth records. Further, I asked if anyone knew anyone pregnant in Savannah, Georgia, in 1980. My fantasy was that my Facebook posts would draw out Adele to contact me.

I received several messages from people who said they remembered a girl in high school who was rumored to be pregnant and hiding her condition. Each responded with the same name: Adele Gibson.

****

The rumors about Adele yielded more information. A much older guy named Jack was presumed to be her boyfriend at the time of my birth. No one could remember his last name so for now, that was a dead end. But another new lead emerged when a woman named Ellen Shaw messaged me on Facebook, "I would love to speak with you privately."

Ellen had lived next door to the home where I was found, and she was grateful for the opportunity to speak with me. She shared her recollections of that long-ago cold March night. Ellen believed that I belonged to the youngest Gibson daughter, Adele, who had a boyfriend named Jack Collins. Jack! Collins! The dots on the family diagram were slowly beginning to connect.

Ellen and I spoke extensively, and she was an invaluable source of information. Between ancestry.com and Facebook.com, a picture of my familial history was emerging. Further research led me from Jack Collins to Jordan Collins, who was his son by his ex-wife. I looked up Jordan online and saw a photo that could only belong to one person: my sibling. Looking at this picture of my half-brother was like looking at a male version of myself.

The focus of my research narrowed again as I investigated Jordan Collins. I searched his Facebook contacts and cross-referenced them on ancestry.com. There were no direct links, but I noticed that Jordan and Adele were Facebook friends, along with many of their family members.

Next, I did the worst possible thing. I messaged Jordan through Facebook and asked him to contact me about a personal matter. He responded logically, "if I don't know you personally, why on earth would I speak with you about a personal matter?" I answered that I just had a few questions I preferred not to post on social media and gave him my phone number. The phone immediately rang. I was terrified. Had I really just messaged a random guy to say that he was my half-brother? That is exactly what I had done!

I took some deep breaths, introduced myself, and told Jordan my story. There was complete silence on his end. So I launched into an explanation of why I thought we were related and asked if he knew Adele Gibson. Jordan finally broke his silence, "yes, I do. I think she and my father were together for a long time before he met my mother." I asked Jordan if he would be willing to take a DNA test with me, one that I would happily pay for. I explained that I had spoken in person to Adele, who denied she was my mother. But DNA told a different story.

I kept on talking breathlessly to Jordan, "I understand if you never want to talk to me again. I understand if you think I am just a random crazy person. Please don't tell anyone that we have spoken because I don't want to make false accusations. But please, you are the only chance I have." Jordan was silent again during my monologue. Finally, he spoke and asked to think about this for a while. He also asked me to send some photos so he could see for himself if we resembled each other. As the conversation wrapped up, I promised Jordan that I would never contact him again unless he reached out first, and I reminded him about the DNA test. Jordan had my phone number and Facebook information (I gave him my real profile account) and I had visions of a wonderful family reunion.

When I saw that a text message from an unknown phone number, my heart skipped. The text read:

> *Kate, ok. You are reaching into people's lives that ultimately is going to only disrupt and hurt others. This is between me and you so let's give you the closure that you say you need. A decision was made to benefit you at the time and opening this door to the past has no benefit to you or your family and certainly not my aging parents.*
>
> *There's absolutely no information I can provide about your medical*

history. I ask that you respect my wishes and for your word that with this closure we can move on with our own individual lives.

My response:

Can I ask who this is? Without knowing whom I am speaking with, I have NO answers or closure.

The final reply:

Adele.

****

At least I had the answer to my primary question: I knew that Adele was my biological mother. I should have been relieved, but I still felt unsettled. The way in which she told me the truth was very hurtful. She wanted nothing further to do with me. Then I chided myself. What did I expect? I had circumvented her and potentially caused a lot of damage. Still, I could not stop crying.

When I gave Ethan the news, he responded, "well, Kate, now you have your answer." I inferred that Ethan was relieved that I would no longer be preoccupied with the search for my biological family. But at that moment, I realized that the answer was only partly what I sought. I had really wanted my mother to want me, to accept me, and to build a bond with me. I must confess that I am now embarrassed by the response I wrote to Adele:

> *Thank you for your honesty this time around. All of this could have been avoided if you had just been willing to speak with me the first time. All I wanted was a simple answer. I'm assuming that your text is a confession that you and Jack are my birth parents. I was really looking forward to a happy reunion, just to get to know you. Rest assured I want nothing material from you.*
>
> *Why couldn't you be honest? I will never understand. Don't worry, your secret is safe. I will take down my Facebook page. I still would like to get to know my half-brothers if they are willing. As for you, I will never ever contact you again.*
>
> *If you have a change of heart, please contact me. I have no intention of*

publicizing this. It is our business and no one else's.

Adele continued the text chain, each message less hostile but certainly not friendly:

Kate, please understand that I never meant to hurt you in any way. Some things are better left alone. I did what I thought was best for you. Jack is not a part of this. Maybe one day I can find the strength to tell you everything. But until then, you need to find peace with your life.

I interpreted Adele's text as a window to a future

relationship and could not stop myself from pressing

further:

Adele, I know you never meant to hurt me. I understand that you were very young and scared. I also know that you did what you thought was best. I have a wonderful life ... Thank you for coming clean to me. I will never reveal anything to your parents or anyone else. Like you, I don't want anyone else to get hurt.
I will honor your wish and give you my word to leave you alone. Please know that is what hurts the most. Not having any relationship with you — even a distant one. I still believe that

Jack is my father. We really look alike, and so do Jordan and me. I may have no siblings born to you, but Jack might.
This is your story, but this is my life. I think everyone deserves to know who their family is. I don't expect you to understand my burning need to know. But trust me, it is difficult and confusing.

That was the end. I regretted being impulsive and relying on rumors and backdoor channels. I felt terrible for the mess I had made and sad that the result was not what I had hoped. I had to be content with just knowing who my biological mother was and having met her once. I made a promise not to pursue the matter – a promise that I found impossible to keep.

It may have been irrational, but I could not control myself from digging further. Even though I had taken down the Mary Doe Facebook page, I still compulsively scoured ancestry.com. My efforts finally paid off again, as I received a message from the username "kg007." The genetic matches on ancestry.com were continually updated, and I saw that kg007 was a new link to me. Not only that, kg007 was listed as an immediate family member!

I agonized about my promise to Adele that I would not contact anyone. But oh, how I wanted to respond to this message! Ethan resolved my dilemma with the answer I had hoped for. He reminded me that I had promised not to *initiate* contact but did not stipulate that I would not *respond* to inquiries. So with shaking hands, I dialed kg007's phone number, and an elderly man answered.

He introduced himself as Keith Gibson, someone new to the ancestry.com site. He had just received his DNA results, and my name was at the top of his list. Mr. Gibson went on, "young lady, I have no idea how we may be related because I know all of my immediate family members. But maybe you can help me. I have three daughters, only one of whom is still living." Before Mr. Gibson told me his daughter's name, I started sobbing. I knew what he would say next. "Her name is Maxine Gibson."

This was literally a moment of truth. Keith Gibson was my grandfather! Was I willing to tell *him* the truth and reveal my identity? My conscience tugged, and I could not speak. His next words were heartbreakingly kind, "hey now, young lady, don't cry. Whatever it is, it can't be that bad. Do you know how we are related?"

I managed to choke out, "Yes, sir, I do. But I can't tell you. I made a promise to someone very dear to you that I would not speak to anyone in your family."

Mr. Gibson said soothingly, "I certainly understand promises. But if that promise is upsetting you this much, perhaps it would be best to just talk about it. Plus, I would really like to know who you are and how you are related to me."

I was torn because I did not want to hurt his family; I wanted to be a part of it. I *needed* someone who *wanted* to know me. This gentleman sounded so kind, so caring. Maybe he would be delighted with a long-lost granddaughter. If not, what did I have to lose? My birth mother had already cut me off.

So I blurted out, "Mr. Gibson, I am your granddaughter!"

"What? How? Who?

"Remember the little baby who was found on your doorstep? I am that baby, and your daughter Adele is my mother!"

"Wow, *you* are that baby? You are my granddaughter?"

"Yes, sir. I am sure this is not what you expected, and I'm sorry you are finding out this way."

"Sweetheart, I am in total shock. I don't know what to say, but I will tell you this, you made my day! We have years and years of catching up and tons and tons to discuss! No matter what, I will never deny you. You have just made me the happiest man in the world." My heart soared.

Mr. Gibson, my grandfather, and I began to speak daily, and we enthusiastically planned to meet in person. I flew up to his home in Cincinnati, Ohio, by myself on February 19, 2017. Ethan was not in favor of this trip at all; he did not like the idea of my visiting a stranger and staying in his home. But I prevailed.

By this point, I did not think of my grandfather as a "stranger" nor as "Mr. Gibson." Instead, he became a beloved family member. He and my newfound aunt Carole, his sister-in-law who lived nearby, picked me up at the airport. Then we had a joyful, emotional lunch at Cracker

Barrel. For the four days I stayed in his guest room, I felt that I had come home. There were some bittersweet moments, however. The walls of the room were covered with photographs of my mother and her two sisters. Pictures of babies, graduations, family events, and weddings made me wish that I had learned of this family history from my mother.

But my gratitude for finally having some missing puzzle pieces to my identity superseded this regret. My grandfather took me on a tour of the area where he and his then-wife Maxine, my grandmother, had lived. We drove by their childhood homes, the church where they got married, and the house where they raised Adele and her sisters. I was thirsty for this knowledge. I believe that individuals *need* to be known and valued by themselves and by others, and this visit went a long way to fulfilling that need in me.

My grandfather was in his late 70s, and I was in my late thirties when we first met. We each had lifetimes to catch up on — experiences, events, interests, feelings, philosophies, and much more. I learned about his career as a manager at a turbo-technology plant whose company relocated him from Cincinnati to Savannah. Also, I learned that his membership in ancestry.com was a Christmas present, and he had used the site to look up cousins and other distant relatives. He said that it gave him another gift: me.

I was impressed by my grandfather's lovingkindness and his openness and honesty. When I asked him if he had been aware at the time of Adele's pregnancy, he said he had not. In fact, he was upset that she had not come to him and her mother Maxine because they would have been more than just supportive — they would have raised me. Further, he was very distressed by Adele's recent behavior toward me. Her unwillingness to acknowledge me angered him. Although she was only a young teenager when she birthed me, he made no excuses whatsoever for how she handled me – then or now.

****

A few months after meeting my grandfather, an unexpected email from Adele arrived in my inbox:

Hi Kate, I hope you're doing well. I understand that you have built a relationship with my dad, and I hope that is helping you. I understand he reached out to you. My mother also knows about you now. If you feel the need to reach out to her, I will never stand in your way.
I tried to tell you to give me some time to process. I said I hope to one day be able to tell you everything. Kate, you need to understand that even with a lot of counseling, I still cannot remember what happened back then. But I have realized I need to work this through the best I can. This situation has caused me a lot of physical problems that are not your fault. I'm sorry things worked out the way they

did. Maybe one day, we can sit down together. Your choice, Adele

Of course, I responded immediately, and a lengthy email chain followed:

Hi Adele, I hope you are doing well. Yes, your dad and I have built a wonderful relationship over the past couple of months. I am proud to call him grandpa. After he took the ancestry DNA test, he learned that I was a direct family link. Then, he contacted me. Please understand that I did not reach out to him. I was even reluctant to disclose my identity because I told you that I would not seek out anyone.

I have not reached out to your mom and did not plan on doing so. I will let her contact me if she wishes to do so. I am truly sorry for all you have dealt with. It has not been easy for me either. I have suffered severe anxiety and gone through lots of counseling too. I hope that now things are more settled, you will get some relief.

I recognize that I unearthed something you wanted to forget. We were both hurting and probably come off harshly to each other. I am sorry.

I would love to sit down and talk with you. It might be therapeutic for both of us.

I frequently travel to Savannah to visit my niece. Or you are welcome at my home in Atlanta. Or we can meet someplace for coffee. I understand we both love coffee with French vanilla creamer. It's your choice, just let me know. Kate

Hi Kate, Please let me know when you are in Savannah again, and we can meet for coffee ▢ You are right – it might be very therapeutic for both of us. I am on vacation the first week of April and am going to the beach. You are welcome to join me.
As for my mother, your grandmother, I don't think she'll reach out. It's not that she doesn't want you in her life, it's more about protecting me. I feel like I should be the one to take you to her.
She is the most compassionate, forgiving person with a true heart of gold. You both deserve to build some kind of relationship. I really do look forward to seeing you, so please let me know when you are in town. Xo Adele

We continued to write to each other, and the tone of our correspondence became warm and lovely. My mood was buoyant. Not only had I found my biological mother after searching for 20 agonizing years, but she was embracing the idea of developing an adult relationship with me.

The subsequent conversations between Adele and me focused on plans to meet. After much back-and-forth, we agreed on a time and place: Friday, March 31, 2017, my 37th birthday, in Hilton Head, South Carolina. The date was coincidental, but it certainly was symbolic. As if that were not special enough, Adele would have the opportunity to meet Pearl too. Three generations, inextricably linked through biology.

Pearl had a cheerleading competition in Hilton Head, and my parents drove her to the practice there on Friday night. That way, I could drive by myself to gather my thoughts and meet Adele alone at first. I needed time to process my mixed emotions — anticipation, fear, and optimism — and my fantasies and expectations of the encounter.

Our conversation began superficially. After all, we were strangers to each other, united by blood, not shared experiences. As the evening progressed, the talk turned more serious. As Adele had explained in her emails, she was only 15 years old when she gave birth to me and did not remember much about that time. She reiterated that she spent a long time in therapy (as had I) and that her intentions were never to hurt me. I could not help thinking that although that may not have been her intention then, surely, she must realize how hurtful her second rejection was when I reached out to her.

After Pearl's competition on Saturday, I introduced her to Adele briefly, and neither seemed particularly overwhelmed. The most dramatic encounter was between Adele and my father, who graciously said, "Thank you for giving Kate to me – she and Pearl are the best parts of my life." Adele responded, "thank you for caring for them."

Needless to say, it was a tearful exchange, as were our goodbye hugs.

The tone of my relationship with Adele continued to be cordial. After the cheerleading event, I texted her, *"Thank you for coming today. It really meant a lot to me."* Her reply, three short sentences, warmed my heart, *"Thank you for allowing me to be there. I'm glad I came. It meant a lot to me too ▯."*

****

Although the visit with Adele helped recalibrate my equilibrium, Ethan and I were still in counseling together. We had drifted far apart when I was preoccupied with solving the mystery of my ancestry. It took some time in therapy before I shared my fear that I was driving Ethan to have an affair when I was almost exclusively focused on my research. My imagination magnified this thought, and I falsely suspected that he was involved with our next-door neighbor. We were very friendly with Nora and Don Saunders, socializing with them on weekends and getting together for summer barbeques and fall bonfires. The relationship was more than that of neighbors casually waving to each other from the driveway. Our families even had a tradition of spending Christmas Eve together.

Don was easy-going and soft-spoken. Nora was a different story; she was outspoken and always commanded the center of attention. Blonde, pretty, and voluptuous, she was very vocal about her sexuality. Once when we got together with a group of neighbors, the men were outside joking about a woman they would like to sleep with. Nora shifted the conversation to herself, flirtatiously commenting, "I wish when *I* walked down the street, some guy would want to have sex with me." She would also regale the group with provocative stories of her former exploits. For example, she once described the time during college when she was at the gym and ended up sleeping with a stranger who was watching her exercise.

I noticed that Ethan was especially friendly with Nora. My rational mind figured that he was using her as a confidant while he and I were struggling. But my irrational side imagined it was plausible they were having an affair. To prevent this from happening, I decided – without consulting Ethan – that we should move across town. Unbeknownst to him, I began house-hunting, found a great home situated in an excellent school system for Pearl, and purchased it. I presented Ethan with the signed real estate closing documents. It was a fait accompli. I was moving with him or without him. Fortunately, we moved as a family.

Although I still feared for the state of my marriage, I was unable to stop myself from communicating with my birth parents. A month or so after meeting Adele on my birthday, she surprised me with an invitation. Adele asked if

Pearl and I would like to join her at the beach on May 12, 2017, to celebrate her mother's 75th birthday. I was pleased that she was fulfilling a promise to facilitate my contact with Maxine, and I jumped at the opportunity. Adele wrote back:

> *That's great! My mother will be so surprised and happy to finally meet you and Pearl! Not sure when you will arrive, but maybe we could find some girl stuff we would all enjoy — pedicures, lunch, trip to the aquarium? Is Ethan coming?*

I welcomed the tone of this note, but it stung to read that Maxine considered this beach trip our first introduction. After all, she had met me long ago on her front lawn and later, inside her home.

The weekend went smoothly, and Pearl thoroughly enjoyed Maxine's attentions. They baked a cake together and goofed around with iPhone photo filters. And Adele live-in boyfriend of 14 years, Clyde, was quite taken with Pearl too. They shared an interest in garage sales and junk, and Maxine called them "two peas in a pod." After Pearl

and I arrived home, I received this lovely email:

> *Kate, I hope you made it home safely. Thank*
> *you so much for coming for mom's birthday.*
> *She so enjoyed us spending time together.*
> *Sorry I forgot to wish you a happy Mother's*
> *Day. I am kind of new at this, so please be*
> *patient ⏷ I know that you will be in Hilton*
> *Head in June with your parents. If I fly my dad*
> *in, will you be able to make time to see him*
> *then? Adele*

My birth mother and I were slowly building a friendship. It

was not a mother-daughter bond, but it was a good start.

I have never enjoyed a positive relationship with

my adoptive parent, Patricia, so I deeply yearned for a

mother and everything I imagined she would offer. I was

never blessed with such a connection naturally; instead, it

required time and hard work. I felt a little bit like the baby

bird searching relentlessly for a mother in P.D. Eastman's

children's book, *Are You My Mother?* The bird's quest was

worth it, and I was confident mine would be too.

Another momentous mother-daughter occasion arose in the summer of 2017. Adele invited me to spend her birthday weekend at her beach house in Hilton Head. I was beyond excited, and, characteristically, I gave the milestone a great deal of thought. I even crocheted a blanket designed with sea turtles, the theme of Adele's house. Giving her a handmade gift meant a lot to me because it expressed my delight and my appreciation that she was now a part of my life. Additionally, we started to bond over our shared interests in crafts and gardening.

We spent most of that weekend talking, enjoying the sun, and cooling off with orange Dreamsicle beverages. The drinks quenched my physical thirst, but I still had an insatiable psychological thirst for family information. The more we conversed, the more I needed that refreshment. At first, any conversation about my biological father Jack and half-brother Jordan was superficial. I was hesitant to push Adele away by pressing her for too many details. But I craved her permission to reach out to my father.

I wanted to avoid uncomfortableness and approached the subject gently. I asked if my father knew that we were spending time together. "Yes," she answered. I followed up by asking, "How would you feel about my contacting him?" Her reply flooded me with relief, "That is your decision. And I will always be here if you do."

****

As soon as I returned home from the beach weekend, I agonized over how to best word an email to Jack, my biological father. I wrote and rewrote and read and reread the message. Finally, I clicked "send."

Subject: Last Try
Date: October 6, 2017

Hi Jack, I am reaching out to you one last time before closing this chapter of my adoption search. I have thankfully fulfilled almost all of my questions and curiosities. I honestly want nothing from you and expect nothing. As I did with Adele, I just want the opportunity to talk and get to know you. It has been wonderful getting to know her, Keith, and Maxine. As for me, I understand the choices made and harbor no ill feelings toward you or my mother.

I have been to Savannah on multiple occasions to visit my grandmother, flown to Indiana to see my grandfather, and have spent long weekends with Adele at the beach. They are all amazing, loving people who have graciously accepted me into their families and lives. I am grateful for the time we have spent together.

I'm not sure if you are interested in knowing anything about me, but I work for Maritime Insurance as an underwriter. I am married to my best friend Ethan and have one biological daughter, Pearl, who is 12, and a stepson Christian who is 13. We currently live just outside Atlanta and stay busy with the kids and their extracurricular activities.

I have struggled for a very long time with being adopted and spent the better part of my life searching for you and my mother. I was diagnosed at age 22 with cervical cancer and feared never having my own children. Luckily, God blessed me with my beautiful, loving, and smart little girl. She is the only child that I am physically able to have.

It is difficult for anyone who wasn't adopted to comprehend the resulting confusion and troubling sense of not belonging. Although my adopted family has treated me as their own, their love never dulled the insecurities and curiosity of not knowing who I am. Not knowing my family roots, medical history, or a blood relative is extremely painful.

Please accept my heartfelt apology for the way I first went about reaching out to you. Once I had my DNA results and knew that my parents were indeed who I suspected, I was angry because I had asked them for the truth. Instead, I was told I was wrong – that, no, you and Adele were not my parents. It hurt to be lied to and denied. In retrospect, I understand this reaction stemmed from pain and fear, as did my lashing back. I accept that how I went about communicating with you was wrong, and I am sorry.

I have only one request: I would like an opportunity to meet you in person and talk. That's all, but it would mean the world to me. I know that Jordan is my half-brother and would love to meet him too. I am an only child and always dreamed of a sibling. If you and Jordan choose not to have a relationship with me, I will respect that decision and let you be. Please, all I am asking for is to meet you once. I would love to build a relationship but understand if that's too much to ask. I am thankful that my mother has accepted me, and we are developing a friendship. It is more than I ever thought I would have.

If you choose to have nothing to do with me, would you kindly respond with a simple "no." That way, I will not be anxiously waiting for a meeting that will never happen. Also, if you choose not to contact me, would you please let Jordan know about me and let him decide if he wants to know me or not?
Sincerely, Kate

Two days later, I received a reply from Jack that generated a brief exchange between us:

Kate, so maybe next time you are in town we can talk. I'll probably provide you with a different perspective.

Hi Jack, I will be in Savannah next Saturday, the 14th. I'm going to help my niece with her wedding preparations. I will arrive Saturday and leave early Sunday morning. If you are available Saturday evening, I could meet you.

Kate, Saw your email. Sorry for the delay in responding. I am swamped on Saturday and don't want to cut you short. I think it's best if I am not running in ten different directions. Best I tell you when I can make it. Also, please do not plan a special trip; only come when it fits your schedule.

Jack was obviously blowing me off. The cycle of reaching out and being rejected was all too familiar to me. What was I expecting? My initial overtures to Adele and Jordan were all met by lies and denials. Why would Jack behave any differently? I represented an embarrassing, painful truth that people did not want to acknowledge. I engaged in self-pity for a while. But I reminded myself of how I had succeeded in establishing rapports with my biological mother and grandfather by being pleasantly but unrelentingly tenacious. I refused to give up on my biological father.

I shared with Adele my correspondence and frustration with Jack. Imagine my delight when she volunteered to reach out to him herself. Not only had my biological mother accepted me, but she was also intervening to help. She was both respecting me and protecting me. Adele contacted Jack and then emailed me:

Subject: Hope this helps
Date: September 27, 2017

Hi Kate, Below is the email I sent to Jack.

Subject: Ancestry results
Jack,
See below, ancestry results. I'm not sure why
you will not respond to Kate. She doesn't
want anything from you – just to meet you
and Jordan. I don't understand how you can
tell me to open up, tell my parents, and quit
hiding and running. Well, I did! Why don't
you do the same?

My family knows Kate and has spent time
with her. Don't worry, I will not be involved
with you two meeting. That is between you
and her. You can call, email, or text her. Your
cousin is the one who found her on ancestry
and is asking how she is related or connected
to the Collins family.

Eventually, the truth will come out. I told Kate
I would reach out to you one last time. You
can hate me or ignore me all you want. But
Kate does not deserve to be hated or ignored.
None of this is her fault.

Wow, I thought, what a turn of events. Adele has truly

embraced me and is trying to convince her family to accept

me as well. I asked her how she felt about my contacting

Jordan, and this was her response:

> As for Jordan, that is your choice. I haven't
> heard from him in a couple of weeks. You are
> both in your thirties, and I feel you both are
> adults and can make your own decisions. I
> would not stand in the way of what you
> decide. Jordan has a funny relationship with
> Jack, so I am unsure how he would react or
> communicate with him. He asked me one time
> about you, and I told him I would sit down
> and talk to him, but he never responded. He
> can be a little hotheaded at times like his dad,
> but he has a big heart. Let me know what you
> decide. Also, just a suggestion: Keep your
> email short and to the point. Save some of the
> details in case he decides to reach out. Men
> tend to get lost in long lengthy emails. Ask
> Ethan. ▨

I was happy that Adele did not disapprove of my

intention to contact Jordan and appreciated her advice. But

it is not my style to write brief emails, so this is what I sent:

> Hi Jordan, I know the first time I contacted
> you caught you off guard. Again, please let
> me apologize. I handled that the wrong way.
> As I told you before, Adele is my mother, and
> I am sure that Jack is my father. I completed
> an Ancestry DNA test that proves I am in his
> direct bloodline. I have also reached out to

Jack through email, and he had agreed to meet with me. That meeting has never happened, and I haven't heard from him since. For some reason, he does not want anything to do with me, nor does it appear that he wants me to contact you. I have waited a year since speaking with you and emailing Jack. I wanted to give him a chance to tell you himself or to reach out to me. He has chosen not to do either.

I'm sure there is some reason surrounding my existence that is meant to be kept hidden and secret. As I said in an email to Jack, I understand that maybe he and Adele do not want everyone to know I exist, and that's fine. However, my only request was to get the opportunity to meet my brother (you).

I honestly do not want anything from the family, nor do I have an ulterior motive. I am the only child of my adoptive parents. My whole life, I wanted so badly to have a sibling. Now, to find out that I actually have a half-brother is very exciting. I am also an aunt. You are an uncle as well. What is one more person to love and spoil all the kids?

After I reached out to you the first time, I know that you contacted your dad because just 24 hours later, I was told to stay out of people's lives. That I was only causing hurt and pain to others. So I am not sure what Jack told you about me or about me being your sister.

Jordan, if you choose not to get to know me, that is your decision, and I will respect it. I will delete your phone number. I just want the decision to be yours, not anyone else's. I want you to know that I am someone who would always be there for you.

Maybe it's just me, and I have some crazy idea about having siblings and bonding with them. I don't know, but I do know that I feel like I have been robbed of knowing you for more than 30 years. So, if you are willing, I want to change that.

I won't ask you not to tell your dad I contacted you because that is unfair, but I know it would only complicate things. He, Adele, and you were the people I most wanted to meet. Adele and I have begun building a relationship, and I have a relationship with her parents as well. I would like to build one with you too.

I only have one favor to ask. Would you PLEASE let me know one way or the other? You can tell me not to contact you again or that you want to get to know me. I promise to respect whatever you decide. If now is not the right time, please know that my door is always open for you. Whether it be tomorrow, six months, or six years from now, I will be here.
Sincerely, Kate

I waited three months for a response...

****

In the meantime, Ethan, Pearl, and I gathered with Maxine, Adele, Adele's boyfriend, Clyde, over Thanksgiving. I was a little apprehensive about how Ethan and Adele would get along. Ethan's communication style is open, and Adele's is closed. I was concerned that Ethan might unknowingly ask about something sensitive like, "Why did you leave Kate on a doorstep? What on earth were you thinking?" Thankfully, Adele and Ethan's interactions were pleasant and friendly. Overall the weekend went well, except for one awkward and upsetting moment, which was not between the two of them. Adele and I went to the grocery store to pick up some last-minute Thanksgiving ingredients. There, she bumped into a friend and introduced me as "an old friend." A friend? Really? It was evident that Adele would not or could not acknowledge me publicly. Her comment was hurtful, and I felt a flash of rejection again as if I were an embarrassing, dark secret.

Finally, in July of 2018, I heard from my half-brother Jordan, who still lives in Savannah, where we were born. I had no idea why, after all this time, he decided to connect. I was worried that something horrible transpired that I did not know about. But I quickly put away my anxiety and became cautiously optimistic. My worries were unfounded; after Jordan contacted me, we developed a sibling bond that I had missed my entire life. We both marveled that at our ages – he was thirty-two and I was thirty-eight – we had discovered each other. Now he and I speak frequently on the phone and try to meet at least once a month for lunch.

In 2017, when the email communications about me between Jordan and his parents heated up, Jordan confronted Adele about my existence. Although she is not his biological mother, she essentially raised him with Jack during weekends, summers, and vacations. When Jordan asked Adele, "Why didn't you ever tell me about Kate? Don't you think I deserved to know I have a half-sister?" Adele responded defensively, "When would you like me to have told you?" Jordan's retort was logical, "Whenever I was old enough to understand." A serious argument ensued, and their rift has never healed. Sadly, the beginning of my relationship with Jordan turned out to be the end of my relationship with Adele. I have not heard from her since then.

Jordan and I have a theory as to why Adele cut off both of us. The seeds of this drama were sown long, long ago. Adele and my father Jack were together in high school but broke up when she graduated. Soon after, Adele married someone else, and six months later, they divorced. Jack also married, and he fathered Jordan, then divorced when Jordan was just two years old. But Adele and Jack were the proverbial couple that could not live together but could not live apart. Their relationship continued until very recently; it ended when I came into the picture.

As I reflect on my biological family's history, it seems like the plot of a long-running soap opera. But it could not be more real. After their respective divorces, Adele and Jack became romantically involved again even though she was simultaneously having an affair. Adele's lover was Clyde, an older man who was her boss at the medical laboratory where she worked. Unbeknownst to Jack and Clyde, Adele was involved with both men when I resurfaced in 2017. Jordan and I theorized that my appearance exposed the truth about these two relationships and ruined Adele's duplicitous romantic life. The downfall came after I made a simple, casual remark.

When Jordan and I reconnected, I would stay with Adele and Clyde during my visits. I innocently mentioned the arrangement to Jordan. He was stunned to learn that his de facto mother was involved with both men. "Clyde?" he asked, "the boss she used to date? That's not the story she told me!" In fact, Adele was still sleeping with Jack while she was living with Clyde. Jordan confronted Jack, who then angrily confronted Adele. Like a made-for-TV Lifetime movie, the damage had a ripple effect on all the characters: Jack and Adele have had nothing to do with each other for over four years. Jack and Jordan have a strained father-son relationship. Jordan and Adele are no longer talking to each other. My biological father, Jack, and I have still never even spoken. And Adele and I have no contact anymore, and I do not expect that we ever will. Apparently, our recent connection was tenuous and meant little to her. Her affairs with Jack and Clyde mattered more. It saddens and puzzles me that Adele, who never had another child, would not want to me — her only baby.

It was difficult to let go of my long-held visions for joyful reunions and adult relationships with my biological mother, father, and half-brother. I had formed idealistic views of the bonds of family. I never considered that finding relatives was entirely different than finding their love. I do not know what is worse: wondering who they were and expecting flawlessness or knowing who they were and experiencing the hurt of a painful reality. Disappointed expectations have led to stress and heartache, but I am grateful that my relationship with my half-brother is one of the exceptions.

My relationship with Jordan now is everything I hoped it would be — and more. Given our years of separation and dramatically different upbringings, our closeness today is remarkable. It seems to underscore the validity of a genetic basis for behavior. Although step-siblings only share 25% of their DNA, compared to 100% for identical twins and 50% for fraternal twins, Jordan and I cannot escape our biology. We have an uncanny ability to sense each other's thoughts and feelings. In this respect, we resemble twins who demonstrate the phenomenon of twin telepathy, whereby the siblings intuit each other's thoughts and feelings, sense if the other is in danger or feeling joy, and mirror facial expressions and body language. When Jordan and I walk side-by-side, our steps and posture are completely in sync. We find ourselves sitting next to each other on the couch and notice we are in the exact same position. At times, our sixth sense and similarities feel a little eerie, but they are unmistakable. One night, I felt the need to call Jordan because I had an intuition that something was wrong. And indeed, he had been in a minor car accident that day.

Jordan and I also seem to think and process information the same way. For example, one time when I was visiting him, my car broke down. People reacted differently in that commonplace situation, but our response was identical. Our focus was not on repairing the car. Instead, we both entirely concentrated on figuring out how I would get home to my family, who lived a 3-1/2-hour drive away. Additionally, we share many of the same interests, including boating, parasailing, and traveling. Perhaps best of all, Jordan has shared his love for our birthplace, Savannah, with me. When I began to visit him there regularly, he always had a thoughtful plan for our activities, choosing sites to show me, making restaurant reservations, and arranging adventures. With Jordan as my guide in my native city, I have developed a deep attachment to Savannah, its culture, history, and landscape. Now, my memories include

Savannah's omnipresent live oak trees surrounded by moss, along with the acorn-producing tree of my childhood.

Of course, there are ways in which Jordan and I are different, but that is true for all siblings. One of the primary dissimilarities between us is how we deal with anger, which I think is a function not of our shared biology but of our divergent nurturing. Jordan did not grow up in a stable home as I did. He believes that his mother (Jack's ex-wife) is bipolar and suffers from attention deficit hyperactivity disorder. Nor did Jordan create a calm home environment during his brief marriage to Cindy, the mother of his two sons, Hank and Alan. In fact, there were rumors of the police being called there to mediate domestic disturbances.

Unlike Jordan, my home life was loving, calm, and predictable. Further, I followed a good path: I went to college, had a daughter, got married, gained a stepson, had a stable job, and lived in a nice house. I achieved all this despite poor health, physical disability, and bouts of depression and anxiety. Added to these challenges was the nagging uncertainty about my parentage. Although I am far from wealthy, I enjoy the comforts of love and stability, and my material needs are more than adequately met. In contrast, the members of my biological family took a different path. They married right after high school graduation, had children, did not attend college, and had jobs, not careers.

As a result of his upbringing, Jordan is more apt to dwell on his past and let it interfere with his present. Understandably, he resents the instability and financial hardships of his early life. However, at times he uses his history to explain, even excuse, his behavior. When I am angry, I focus on finding solutions. My anger motivates me to move forward, whereas Jordan's tendency is to look back. And sometimes, Jordan's anger fuels his drinking. I suspect that Jack, my father and Jordan's, has a history of alcoholism.

As with any siblings, we have endured some strained periods in our relationship. When Jordan drinks, he becomes needy and calls me repeatedly. However, I have learned to set limits, refusing to speak with him when he is out of sorts. And gradually, Jordan is learning to respect my boundaries. He understands that I have absolutely no tolerance for alcoholism. Given my history with Gregory, who drank and did drugs, and my experience of being hit and maimed by a drunk driver, I cannot condone such behavior. Accordingly, I do not drink, except perhaps a sip of wine on a special occasion.

****

I recognize all the blessings I have received and sometimes wonder why I ever felt so desperately that my life was lacking. But the fact is, rightly or wrongly, I had experienced a deep sense of insecurity and otherness that motivated me to search for my birth family. It was not because my adoptive parents did not cherish me; they most certainly did. They provided me with every advantage and raised me to attend a Southern Baptist church every Sunday and participate in youth social activities. Although I have moved away from organized religion and its practices, I remain deeply spiritual, with an abiding faith in God. If you are a good person and do good works, I believe God is looking out for you. That is the core principle I wish to instill in my daughter Pearl.

Another value I hold dear is that of hard work. Despite the turmoil of my personal life, I have worked as an assistant underwriter for the same company, Maritime Insurance, for over ten years. Rather than becoming too distracted to focus on work, the job has proved to be a welcome respite from the turbulent ride with my birth family. I am hyper-focused at the office and maintain the high quality of my work. I love my job and cherish my friendships with colleagues. Also, I have developed a core group of female friends with whom I go out to dinner every week. We have supported each other through a lot of personal drama. My relationship with Alissa, who began work at Maritime Insurance at the same time I did, has been exceptionally close. I have shared the intimate details of my struggles and successes with her. Alissa is about fifteen years older than me and has had her own challenges. She is a single mother, and along with her teenagers, she is raising two grandchildren — a middle schooler and a preschooler. Ethan is so appreciative of her friendship with me that he once sought her out to thank her directly.

It can sometimes be difficult juggling what Jordan calls my "now family" with my newly acquired family. Although I love him dearly and will always be there for him, the truth is that Ethan, Pearl, and my adoptive parents do come first. Their needs take priority. I have worked hard to nurture my marriage and continue to do so. Too many times, my search for my birth family drove a wedge between Ethan and me, but we have continually worked hard to heal our relationship. Also, Pearl is a teenager now, and at this stage, our mother-daughter relationship needs careful attention. My parents are in their late 70s and dealing with declining health – my father is blind, and my mother is an obese insulin-dependent diabetic. Since I keenly feel that I lost most of my biological family, I am very conscious of holding the rest of my family close. After years of yearning for what I lacked, I am especially mindful of appreciating the treasures I do have.

Among these treasures are my grandfather, who physically and emotionally accepted me with open arms when we connected years ago through ancestry.com.

Grandpa, my Aunt Carole, and her daughter, Donna, all live on the same 80 acres of farmland in Somerville, Ohio. It is a working farm that grows soybeans and corn, where my grandfather grew up and married. He now rents the land to local farmers, but he and Aunt Carole each maintain homes on the property. Aunt Carole was married to grandpa's brother, Gabe, who passed away some time ago. Grandpa and Aunt Carole are examples of how biological ties are not the only ones that bind family; their relationship is as close as a brother and sister. And Aunt Carole has become like a beloved grandmother to me. As we rock on her porch and chat, she shares her wisdom with me, and I feel like I have come home.

Ethan, Pearl, and Christian share my fondness for Aunt Carole and cousin Donna and immensely enjoy our visits. Aunt Carole is always ready with a handwritten welcome note and the cookies and sweet tea we love. She has her John Deere Gator readied with gas for Pearl and Christian, who spend their days there driving around the farm and exploring. Ethan also enjoys the freedom on the farm, occupying hours by looking for arrowheads in the fields and amassing quite a collection of them. And Somerville itself is a friendly, small town that reminds me of Andy Griffith's Mayberry.

Aunt Carole and Donna have been highly instrumental in deepening my understanding of my mother and her childhood. Maxine and Carole were once extremely close, as were Adele and Donna. But those relationships were destroyed when Maxine and Adele found out that my grandfather had told Carole and Donna about me. It enraged both my biological mother and grandmother that their heavily guarded secret about my birth was exposed. In sharp contrast, Carole and Donna have stood by me. They do not dismiss my feelings of anger, loss, and betrayal. On the contrary, they validate me.

I have gained valuable insight into Maxine and Adele that does not excuse their behavior towards me but does help explain it. Maxine had a hellish life. Her mother killed herself when she was very young. And if that were not enough to bear, her father, a ladies' man, abandoned her and her brother in a hotel room in Las Vegas. It seems like this side of the family has no qualms about throwing away relationships. Social services intervened, and Maxine and her brother went to live with another family member and were constantly being shuffled around.

Maxine had three daughters with my grandfather, but Adele is the only one still alive. Perhaps Maxine is incredibly protective of Adele because of losing everyone else in her family. But ironically, she has chosen to no longer communicate with grandpa, Carole, and Donna. In so doing, she suffers a self-inflicted loss.

****

I have gained many wonderful wished-for family members through my husband's family and my grandfather's family. Perhaps a special present, however, is something that you had not even thought to expect. I had never really considered the role of my foster parents. They were the ones who brought me into their home when I was discharged from the neonatal intensive care unit as a five-week-old preemie and lovingly cared for me for 7-1/2 months. Although I had not been searching for them, I learned in 2021 that they had been searching for me for over twelve years.

Using a nonprofit volunteer organization called Search Angels, they were finally able to track me down. The telephone numbers they were given belonged to each of my adoptive parents. When they called my mother, she promptly hung up, believing the call was some kind of scam. My father hung up on them too, but he had an inkling that the callers had used a legitimate ancestry registry. So he called me, saying that I should phone the number on his caller ID because they might have been my foster parents. My father knew how much I wanted to discover my family roots and advised me it was worth trying.

The first time we spoke, the couple identified themselves as Sharon and Walter Wilson, and we had a lengthy conversation. They knew me as "Mary," the name I was given when discharged from the hospital. We needed to find a way to verify that I indeed had been their foster child. Fortunately, a picture among those given to my adoptive parents by social services included one of my foster parents and me together. When Sharon heard this news, she excitedly asked me to send it. I immediately took a screenshot with my phone and texted the photo to her. The following spoken words on the phone were ecstatic, as Sharon cried and screamed to her husband, "It's Mary! I found Mary!"

We Facetimed and planned a trip to meet in June, and they insisted that they would drive from their home in Alabama to Atlanta. Then Sharon called me right back, asking if we could meet sooner. "Kate, I don't want to scare you or push you away," she explained, "but I can't wait to meet you. I've missed you so much!" So they came the very next weekend, and our reunion was wonderful.

Sharon and Walter came laden with precious remembrances: my hospital bracelet reading "Baby Girl," my fetal heart monitor, going home outfit, baby picture, and a handwritten progress report Sharon wrote to social services. These were all items I had imagined my birth parents would have provided. But who gave them to me does not matter now; what matters most is that I finally possess tangible objects dating back to the earliest moments of my life. The items were evidence of my identity! My joy was multiplied by the thought that although I once was discarded like a used tissue, someone had valued me enough to save my belongings. This meant that I truly belonged to someone. The Wilsons were also a welcome source of information, sharing details of my appearance, preferences, and developmental milestones. For example, the simple fact of knowing when I first rolled over was incredibly meaningful to me. I finally had an oral history of my earliest months.

Social services had contacted Sharon and Walter when I was two weeks old, asking if they were willing to foster an abandoned, very premature baby who likely had medical issues. They did not hesitate and came to the NICU to meet me, where they stayed by my side for the next three weeks. I was five weeks old when Sharon and Walter took me home in April 1980. I lived with them until what Sharon calls "the dreaded day of October 18th," when social services came to take away "her baby."

Sharon and Walter explained that they had desperately wanted to keep me. They had no children of their own and petitioned the family court to adopt me. They were denied because, at the time, the regulations stipulated that an abandoned baby could not be adopted by anyone affiliated with the social services department, including foster parents. Apparently, there was a risk that the biological mother would return to claim the baby. Further, my adoptive parents were already next in line on a waiting list for adoption, so I was placed with them from foster care.

The Wilsons were so devastated by losing me, they chose not to foster another child. A year later, they adopted a baby girl. Like a small percentage of infertile couples, they were subsequently blessed with children: two biological sons. Sharon and Walter have always said that they have four children, as they count me as one of their own. They report that I was extra-special because I was their first.

The next time I saw the Wilsons, I drove by myself to their house in Alabama and stayed with them. It is an understatement to say that the experience was emotional. On a prominent wall in their home, there was a gallery of family photographs. The Wilsons had pictures of their children's milestones: birth, graduations, marriages, and holidays. And there was a family collage that included me as a baby, which was the first portrait of my foster parents and me. Sharon insisted that she add snapshots of my life, including my wedding picture and photos of Pearl and Christian. I am literally on the wall like one of their own children. There was no way I could have known before this encounter that they were so invested in me.

During my first visit, I met one son, their adopted daughter, and Facetimed their other son. It was mindboggling that I had gained so many family members over the span of a few years. I kept thinking I had spent most of my life seeking people who didn't even care if I was alive, and these people spent twelve years searching for me. Suddenly, my world had expanded by additional parents, grandparents, aunts, uncles, cousins, and a half-brother.

Sometimes, I wish that I were not so concerned about other people's feelings. When I shopped for father's day cards in 2021, I spent an excessive amount of time in the aisle pondering what to buy. I consider my adopted father as my "real" father. Since my early childhood when we planted acorns, he has been an extraordinary and supportive presence. But I also bought cards for my husband, father-in-law, biological grandfather, and foster dad. I went from growing up in a family of three to having an overwhelming number of family members.

Along with these new relationships came expectations that at times, have proven challenging. Although I dearly love my half-brother, he can be demanding and jealous of my "now family." Similarly, my foster parents are lovely and loving and want me to view them as my "other parents." They invite me to holidays, such as Thanksgiving, Christmas, and family vacations, and feel excluded when I spend those occasions with my adoptive parents. Much like I thought that I was betraying James and Patricia when I searched for my biological parents, I feel like I am betraying everyone else when I prioritize my adoptive parents, husband, and children.

Nevertheless, I continue to celebrate holidays with my immediate family. We have lifelong traditions, and my relationships go beyond loyalty. Our mutual love is deeply rooted. I am again reminded of the strong oak tree in my childhood backyard, which perfectly symbolizes our bond.

****

Occasionally, I reflect on what it is like for my daughter Pearl not to know her biological father. Gregory had visited her once when she was seven weeks old, obviously too young for her to remember. Then, concerned about his drug use and other unsavory behavior, I petitioned the probate court to force Gregory to relinquish his parental rights. He did not fight the petition and did not ask to see her again. My husband Ethan, who met Pearl when she was a toddler, is the only father she has ever known. And they love each other as if they were genetically related.

My own experiences informed how I handled the effect on Pearl of the absence of her biological father. When she was five years old, I told Pearl about Gregory, not wanting her parentage to be shrouded in mystery like mine had been. I also did not want her feeling untethered to her identity. So I made clear that if she ever wanted to contact Gregory, she had my blessing.

Meanwhile, I discovered that Gregory got married. His now-ex-wife claimed he perpetrated domestic violence, and she divorced him. He has been in and out of prison since we broke up when I was in my mid-twenties, and I learned he finally was released three years ago. This is further confirmation that I was wise to become Pearl's sole legal parent.

When Pearl was twelve years old, out of the blue, Gregory wrote to her. Pearl asked my permission to write back, which I readily encouraged. In her letter, she described herself and detailed her passion for high school and competitive cheerleading. Somewhat surprisingly, Gregory wrote back. But unsurprisingly, he had not paid careful attention to the letter; he asked how her dance lessons were going. Pearl felt dismissed and disgusted, saying, "I don't need to know him. I don't want to know him. He doesn't even take an interest or listen to me. He could have written before now and never did." They have not communicated since.

Relationships depend on sharing information, experiences, and feelings; they are built by communication. The journey I described in this book is rooted in the morass of the unknown. But as I discovered, knowing the identity of my birth parents did not generate the kind of relationships I had wished for nor imagined. Not only was I abandoned at birth, but I also felt rejected a second and third time, forsaken again by both my biological mother and father. But my search also gave me some beautiful gifts, including lovely relationships with my biological grandfather and his extended family. I also received a surprise present when my foster parents found me, and we established a bond.

I cannot reiterate enough times how much I value Patricia and James, my adoptive parents. Perhaps it is unnecessary to call them "adoptive." They *are* my parents and gave me the love, the support, and the family unit that every child deserves. They have nurtured, embraced, and loved me unconditionally through illness, injury, failed relationships, and more. Blood and DNA did not make my family – Patricia and James Peters did.

Most important of all is the family I have created: my daughter Pearl and my husband, Ethan. After my cervical cancer at a young age, I feared being unable to have a biological child. I mourned the loss of this possibility. My daughter, Pearl, is an unexpected treasure. And my marriage to Ethan has completed my immediate family and gave me my stepson Christian. For all of you, I am eternally grateful.

Epilogue

Adoption is a complicated issue that affects many individuals and families. Of course, there is the central triad: the birth parents, adoptive parents, and adoptee. But there are many others involved, including social service agency personnel, extended family members, and possibly attorneys.

According to dictionary.com, the word "adoption" is more than a legal designation; it also describes a choice, i.e., the act of accepting or embracing something [or someone] as your own. An important message for adoptive parents to impart is that you and your child are now a "forever family" and that s/he will always be well-loved and cared for.

There are two types of adoptions, open and closed, and each presents its own challenges. Open adoption means that the identity of the birth parents is known to the adoptive family, and there can be contact between them before and after the legal adoption. In contrast, a closed adoption means that the parties' identities are confidential, so there can be no communication between them. The language of the legal terms and conditions of adoption – open versus closed – aptly describes the ease or lack thereof of accessing information and forming family relationships. Consequently, there is a difference in the nature of the psychological impact on the adoptee. As the party to a closed adoption, the mystery that shrouded my biological parentage caused me to feel deeply insecure and unwanted. However, many adoptees are not troubled by this mystery and do not become detectives like me.

My own experiences are just that: mine and mine alone. However, I have networked with other adoptees, and many of us share similar feelings and experiences attributable to being adopted.

- Loss: Adoptees experience multiple losses, including a loss of identity and self-esteem, abandonment, and the absence of genealogical, genetic, and medical history.

- Anger: Our losses fuel anger, raising the question: how could you possibly not want me? The immediate family of the adoptee may also feel anger that their well-loved child is focusing on a search for other family members, rather than loving and accepting their adoptive ones.

- Guilt: This can take two forms: We feel guilty that we did something wrong that caused us to be rejected. And there is concern that when we search for our biological family, we are betraying our adoptive parents who love us. If we undertake a secret search thinking we are protecting them, we may feel even more ashamed about our behavior.

- Acceptance: Personally, I have never once felt ungrateful for my terrific adoptive parents nor for the privileged life I have led. I cannot emphasize this sentiment enough. But I have had to make peace with the fact that the fantasies I once had about reuniting with my birth family were, for the most part, unfulfilled.

Different feelings arise at different developmental stages of an adoptee's life. Here are some of the emotions I coped with:

- As an elementary school child unable to complete a family tree, I had the discomfort and embarrassment of being different.

- When I turned 18 years old and could legally access my birth records, I felt jubilant anticipation followed by disappointment.

- Whenever I had a medical issue, I obsessed about and feared not knowing critical background information.

- When I worked in a pediatrician's office, I felt jealous of the babies whose moms were cooing over their resemblance to a relative.

- When I gave birth to my daughter as a single parent and gained sole parental rights, I worried about her not knowing her father.

- As an adult, I have wondered if the fact that I was adopted impacted my decisions.

There is a plethora of excellent resources available to help with any adoption-related issue. Whether you want to know about how to adopt a child from overseas, or how to tell your child she is adopted, or the legal steps involved with the process, or how to get a DNA test, or other topics — there is readily accessible information to answer your questions. There are also professionals and organizations more than willing to assist you. For me, there is also great value in talking with other adoptees. **No one in the triad of birth parents, adoptive parents, or adoptees needs to face their challenges alone.**

Acknowledgements

I would like to express my special thanks of gratitude to Melinda Ruben, who enabled me to be able to write my story. This book wouldn't have been possible without her help and expertise.

Made in the USA
Monee, IL
14 December 2021

85268767R10090